To Gemma
Keep 5
Peace + blessings
Abi
x

NATURE'S MEDICINE FOR THE SOUL

A guide to living your life abundantly
using essential gifts from the earth

Abi Osho

10-10-10
Publishing

Nature's Medicine for the Soul
www.soul-medicine.co.uk.
Copyright © 2018 ABI OSHO

ISBN: 9781729127162

Contents

Dedication

Jide, my amazing husband, where do I start?
Thank you for your continued patience, whilst writing my book.
Thank you for lifting my spirits when I started to feel overwhelmed.
Thank you for always sharing your positivity and belief in me.

Morenike and Ezekiel, you are incredible young people,
whom I love and cherish with all my heart.
Thank you, Osho, for being you, for teaching me to be patient with
my new endeavours and for sharing your beautiful space with me,
when I facilitate my natural health & guided meditation classes.
To my wider family and friends, much love always.
The universe belongs to us all;
create and receive what is rightfully yours.

Foreword

Are you living the life of abundance you wish to have? Are you telling your own story or living someone else's? Do you want to find out more about the essential gifts that nature ultimately wants to share with you?

Would you like to discover your purpose on this planet, and become healthier, happier, and wealthier while you tap into the power of nature? Would you like to learn more about the power of meditation? No matter who you are or what your current situation is, regardless of your age, culture, beliefs or religion, this book is full of insights, and will act as a guide in your life, advising you of helpful steps to take as you are going through your own transition and becoming the best version of yourself.

Abi Osho left a career of 20 years to follow her passion, which is natural health. This was a life-changing decision to make, but Abi could no longer ignore her intuitive inner voice. After making the decision to retrain and change her life, and the lives of hundreds of other people, she created her own company called "Soul Medicine." Abi is a true example of what you can become when you apply the methods she teaches you within this book.

From her own experiences, as well as those of her clients, Abi has gained a wealth of knowledge and experience. She has written *Nature's Medicine for the Soul* so that you can learn how to appreciate everything in nature that surrounds you, and turn your challenges into your soul-felt success, just as she did.

Abi shares with you many of her own personal experiences to help you to overcome fear and move to a place of emotional and physical wellbeing. She believes that every day is a new beginning, and you have the power in you to change that which no longer serves you. This guide will help you gain a deeper understanding of yourself through embracing, nature, plant-based medicine, and meditation, while you are on your journey of transformational change.

Raymond Aaron
New York Times Bestselling Author

Acknowledgements

I am humbled and eternally grateful that I have been able to write this book. When I agreed to do this, I recall getting lost in my thoughts about writing this book, I felt somewhat overwhelmed with the whole process, and then I remembered why I was writing it, to share my story with the modest hope that it may inspire you to share your own gifts and talents. It was then that my focus changed, and I knew I had a duty to myself and to you the reader to make it happen, without excuses or apologies.

I always knew that I was easily distracted; however, when writing this book, I took distraction to a whole new level, it took every last part of me to stay focused and concentrate on what I wanted to achieve, and I finally made it.

I want to thank my incredible husband Jide for supporting me, listening to my ideas, early into the morning of the following day, and for always being willing to listen to what I had to say and to give constructive feedback as well as constantly telling me how proud he was of me.

To my brother Osho (this is not a reference to Osho the guru), whose education and knowledge runs as deep as a well that holds infinite amounts of water, thanks for your wise words of wisdom, not just about my book, but throughout my life. I truly appreciate them more than you will ever know.

Donna, we have come such a long way since the age of 12 when we were both in care; it was then that we always said we would be friends, and 39 years later we have stayed true to our word. You are an amazing lady who would still give her last penny to anyone you felt was more deserving of it than you.

Rosemary, thank you for reminding me about the importance of time and friendship; you have been consistent in my life and help me stay grounded, just like a tree.

Elaine, we started our first business together, Natural NRG, over 15 years ago and we have created many other business ventures since that time. You are one of the hardest working women that I know. You are the silent entrepreneur, always seeking to improve your life and that of your lovely daughter Leonie. You are such a great example to her and you continue to flourish and create endless possibilities; your actions speak volumes. To your continued success; I look forward to reading your book.

Michelle, thank you for your understanding, when I changed our plans at the last minute, and for keeping me on track with the writing of my book. You always managed to weave it into our conversations, and helped me keep the vision alive and turn it into a reality.

Jeremy, thank you for taking the time out of your busy schedule to proofread my book; your honest feedback was truly appreciated.

L, thank you for sharing your story of prostate cancer with me; your words were truly heartfelt and I know they will help other people who may be worried about getting checked by their GP.

Finally, thank you Raymond Aaron and team, for supporting me with the creation of my first book.

Chapter 1

You Owe It To Yourself

For years, we have been living in an increasingly artificial world. Many of us have become so accustomed to the concrete that surrounds us in urban areas that what we see all around us is no longer questioned; it has become our normality. We live in the city for convenience of work, transport, restaurants and any other components that form part of the 24/ 7 lifestyle. Urban living has desensitized us from our natural environment.

The unnatural environment that we have created continues to cause hazards to our health; for example, air pollution can cause respiratory disease, heavy metals can cause neurotoxicity, which refers to damage to the brain or peripheral nervous system (including the nerves that lie outside the brain and the spinal cord) caused by exposure to natural or man-made toxic substances. Our global climate is changing, which will affect every species on this planet. It's time to start appreciating our natural environment. Getting closer to nature also helps you on your own journey of self-discovery. Research has shown that embracing our natural environment provides both long and short-term health benefits; for example, relief of stress, depression, ADHD in children, and emotional health.

I was raised in East Sussex, which was full of vast areas of untouched woodlands, and natural brooks that separated the woodlands from the shortcuts to other sections of the town.

Near our house, there were two trees in the woods, that were perfectly made for climbing and enabled me to observe my natural environment. I've seen a squirrel storing its food for the winter, a sparrow sitting on the top branch of a tree singing, and beautiful vibrant coloured butterflies extracting pollen from flowers. I was able to experience this world of nature most days. Nature was introduced to me at a young age, and I remember feeling a great sense of freedom and independence whilst walking through the sprawling woodlands. Therefore, I want to share with you how liberating and meditative nature allows you to be, when you are fully present in the moment.

My journey with essential oils started in Egypt over 27 years ago. Essential oils in the form of pure plant medicine are very powerful, and I believe are true gifts of the earth. The history of essential oils goes as far back as 3000 B.C. The Egyptians used aromatic plants for medicinal and cosmetic purposes, as well as for the embalming of the deceased. Pharmaceutical medicines were introduced in 1869, which is less than 200 years ago. The base ingredient of most conventional medicine is derived from the plant; the remaining components are synthetic, and can cause side effects. They are created to treat a specific symptom in the body. Plant-based medicine's natural response is to find the root cause and help the body repair itself holistically. What I find refreshing is that natural medicine can be taken alongside conventional medicine, and consequently this helps the body maintain its natural balance.

From an early age, I have always been fascinated by the human mind. As a child, I would comfortably sit with the adults and watch numerous documentaries about human behaviours. Whilst I didn't understand the terminology used in the programmes, in my daily life I was constantly observing people's facial expressions, body language, and interpreting for myself what their body language meant to me. Growing up, my fascination expanded into the area of our subconscious mind. I was intrigued by the concept of right brain vs left brain. For example, a person who is "left-brained" is often said to be more logical and analytical. A person who is "right-brained" is said to be more intuitive and thoughtful. I was drawn towards the workings of the right brain. It was through this research that I began to understand the power of our thoughts, emotions and intuition; which I speak about and share with you further into my book.

You may be wondering what any of this information has to do with transforming your life! And if you want to make changes, where do you start? As a person who has transformed my own life, through leaving my career after 20 years, retraining and becoming a natural health coach, executive leadership mentor and clinical hypnotherapist, I know that I have found my purpose. I work primarily, but not exclusively, with women who are on their individual journey of transition, and my gift is re-introducing them to their natural environment and re-igniting their passion through the use of pure essential oils. For example, certified pure Frankincense is highly effective for brain and memory functionality, balancing hormones and boosting immunity. Throughout my book I share many of the highs and the lows of my journey of transition, and how each of my experiences with the natural environment helped shape who I am today. It is my hope that it helps you to get started on your own purpose-driven journey, and ultimately leads you to finding your happiness from within.

Not Everything Is As It Seems

Why is it that most of us try to find ways to hide or erase our imperfections? It seems as if there is always something to work on, always something that is not good enough. We are constantly comparing ourselves to others, invariably focusing on what we believe we are less than.

We are led to believe that to be accepted we need to seamlessly fit into any situation; it could be something simple like we laugh too loud or we weigh 10 more pounds than we would like to, or we don't have the same dress sense as those around us.

It is often the case that when we are accepted for a new job role, the feeling of wanting to fit in, sometimes at any cost, is extremely high. Whilst we have many strengths that qualify us for the new role, usually it is a weakness that the employer will highlight, and, in many situations, we feel inadequate and incapable of fully carrying out the role we so badly wanted in the first place. Sometimes there are comments passed that may sound something like "He wasn't like this when he first started working here." That's because we want to be seen as being perfect; we want to be 10 out of 10 in every area, and this is just not possible, and we end up placing too much pressure on ourselves.

The truth is, and studies have shown, that some individual personality traits are linked to our genetics. Behavioural genetics' study of personality has made it clear that genes are important. In fact, a number of personality traits have been identified as having a genetic basis. Whilst for many people it may seem tempting to work on changing certain personality traits, most of the time this will be based on comments that have been received from another individual, who has highlighted their own opinion of our flaws. However, this is not something that we can change with ease.

In order to fit in we try and change our natural self, to be part of the unspoken social normality that surrounds us. Once we decide something is an imperfection, we often try to hide it, eradicate it, pretend it doesn't exist. In doing so, we create a false image of ourselves to the world. This may cause the feeling of conflict from within, as we know that we are not reflecting who we really are. Invariably we all want to put our best self forward. Remember the one thing that we all have in common is that we all have flaws. None of us are flawless, and that's what makes us such unique human beings. Rather than continually trying to hide your flaws, why not start to embrace them, share them with others, along with your strengths? This is an effective way to introduce internal emotional balance; what I mean by that is that it is also unhelpful to your thought process when you only talk about your flaws. Start thinking about how to create a new daily narrative that reflects who you are, including your imperfections.

The Art Of Being Present

In today's society we constantly hear or are advised to live life in the present moment. What does this really mean? What does it mean to you? When you think about it, life can only be truly lived in the present. So often, we allow the present to slip away. Allowing time to rush past, both unobserved and sometimes unappreciated. We spend so many moments of our lives worrying about the future or getting stuck thinking about what happened in our past. We are living in a world that contributes in a major way to mental fatigue, constant distraction, and increased levels of stress. As humans we're always doing something; we continually feel the need to stay busy, to rise at the crack of dawn and keep going late on into the night, or even into the following morning. We then enter our place of work the following day, proud to share how busy we have been, almost viewing this behaviour like a badge of honour, in terms of who can stay busy for the longest period of time. With this in mind we allow little time to practice stillness and calm. In fact, it's probably furthest from our mind.

Whilst we are at work, we daydream about being on holiday; when we're on holiday we worry about the work piling up on our desk, and how we will cope with the backlog when we're back at work. We dwell on intrusive memories of our past or concern ourselves about what may or may not happen in the future. We've learnt not to appreciate living in the present as our frenetic minds jump from one thought to another, similar to a hamster on a wheel, that continues to go around and round without taking a rest and coming up for air.

As humans, we tell great stories. We like to listen to other people's stories and compare them with our own. In some ways we could say that the entire universe is based on one collection of stories, a universal story. The problem is that we feel the need to create a story about everything we experience, thus our story is never-ending. We confuse the world as it is with the way we think about it, talk about it and describe it. It is only when we realise this that we are able to return to a state of peace and stillness, which will allow us to live in the present.

What we really want is to find balance and start experiencing reality as it is; the challenge we face when living in the moment is trying to quiet our mind. It seems that when we do this our thoughts increase even more. But you may find by simply witnessing your thoughts, and not judging your thoughts, this practice over time will help you to quiet your own mind. Practicing mindfulness, or being present in the moment, means we exercise our awareness in all actions.

It means that your awareness is completely centred on the here and now. You are not worrying about the future or thinking about the past. When you live in the present, you are living where life is happening. The past and future are not real, they don't exist. If being present is a new concept for you, you may wish to start with a simple task like, eating your breakfast in the morning by slowly chewing your food and experiencing the flavours and the sensations that occur throughout the process. You can apply being present to any situation throughout the day. With practise it will become easier for you and, over time, you will start to reap the benefits of a calmer mind, which can lead to decreased levels of stress.

Uncovering Your Abundance

What does abundance mean? We constantly hear people talk about and discuss living abundantly, but what does that mean? This is the Oxford dictionary definition: "Existing or available in large quantities plentiful;" for example, 'the riverbanks were abundant in beautiful wild plants.' The law of abundance is an abiding principle within the universal laws. It's a simple fact that there is an unlimited source of everything we need or could ever want. Think about living your own abundant life; what if you started living out of abundance instead of lack? What if, at the end of the day, you went to bed completely satisfied with what you had accomplished?

Although our world is spinning at a faster and faster pace, and we are constantly pulled in so many directions, we still desire stillness. It's the one thing we have forgotten to cultivate, and instead we feel the need for constant productivity. When we stop, slow down, even focus on one thing at a time, we can see more clearly. We can experience things from a place of contentment rather than striving, and we can find more joy.

Circumstances are always changing; common happiness is fleeting. However, choosing to be grateful for what is good in your life right now creates a new perspective for you. It also allows you to measure your responses to situations, rather than being controlled by your past experiences. When you stay busy surveying your own landscape, instead of constantly comparing it to others, you will notice that which comes from a distorted view of somebody else's reality. You may see someone else's success and assume there isn't enough to go around. That is untrue; each of us is fighting our own battle, and they all look different. When you focus on your own precious life, you start to gain a purer picture of each of your natural gifts. You will notice there is always enough for you.

How many of you look at everything in your life that seems to be holding you back? You constantly focus on self-created limitations, which can leave you feeling powerless. Abundance doesn't mean that you have it all, it doesn't mean that you have everything that you hoped for; it means what you have is sufficient for who you need to be, and what you need right now. What if you started living as if there were enough? Enough money, enough opportunities, enough healing? I'm sure you get my drift. When you cultivate the feeling of gratitude, you are embracing your own abundance, and therefore enhancing the opportunity for endless abundance to surround you.

Discover The Power Of Nature

There are so many items in your life that you must pay for, and even when you earn more money through a pay rise or business growth, it seems to disappear just as quickly as when you received it. What I absolutely love about nature is that you can find it wherever you live, and wherever you work, and it's free. Sometimes I feel that we do not use our wonderful open spaces enough. Find a way to introduce your children to open green spaces as young as possible. I've been to some European countries where there is a charge for entering certain green parks, and it would be a tragedy if this were to happen here, so please remember to use your incredible free open spaces.

Think about this for a minute: when we walk, run or cycle in the park, countryside, woods or forest, not only do we boost our physical health, but as we soak up the sunshine, our body is being nourished with vitamin D. Even just sitting in a natural environment for 5 to 10 minutes a day increases your vitality and emotional wellbeing.

I love our natural environment; it's a place when you can let go of your everyday stresses and various forms of anxiety, and you can even put down your mobile phone or tablet, which may have been glued to your hand and ear for most of the day. I can assure you that the world will not come to an end before your very eyes. Smelling the scent of roses, tree bark and freshly cut grass, listening to the birds sing to each other and watching them fly away to faraway places makes me feel more alive. Your own experiences will probably be different, but you may have had similar feelings.

Nature may be on your doorstep, close to home or in a remote place, but the effect of spending time in nature is the same. Whether it's the blackbird in your garden, or the red and black ladybird that's landed on your table, stop and watch, and truly be in the moment. In connecting with nature, you understand and appreciate it. You care more about preserving animal habitats, as well as recognising that nature provides enjoyment for yourself.

This will not apply to everyone, but when our lives revolve around urban homes, workplaces, shopping areas and leisure centres, we remain detached from our natural surroundings. We can hide from how our food is produced, from environmental damage to our rivers and oceans, from the microplastics that continuously wash up on the sea shores, to the hundreds of rivers that join each other across the country. Progressively, it has become very common of late that you may see plastic bags and water bottles, washed up on the shores of our river banks or seas, spoiling the landscape. This is all our own making.

The natural environment can increase our sense of social responsibility and give us greater satisfaction and purpose. This is a place where our mind, body and soul meet without interruption from the urban world.

Nature At Its Best

I remember walking to the bus stop every day, head down, with what felt like a million thoughts running through my mind about work; what time had I planned this meeting for, who was involved in the meeting, how many staff were going to phone in sick today? Who could I contact to cover their position? How many contracts will I need to sign; how many interviews do I have? I recognise now that I had the same thoughts every day, ruminating in my mind without even realising, or taking notice of anything around me. I would get on the bus and see the same faces each morning and never say a word to anyone.

Until one day, I knew there would be road works on my route for the next two weeks, so I decided to take a different route to the bus stop. I left my house earlier, and as I left home I decided I wanted to know what it was like to be in the moment; so instead of always looking down I looked up, and I vividly remember seeing two green parakeets flying over my head and noticing how blue the sky was. It was a poignant moment for me. I recall asking myself why I never looked up towards the sky, why I always looked down as I walked to the bus stop. I started to observe the trees and the flowers, and I truly heard the birds sing for the first time in a very long time. It was beautifully calming.

Being in nature is the most serene, beautiful, unique experience, and it always has a gift for you and me. Experiencing nature is a great addition to your life. The next time you are bored or stressed, take a break and listen to the birds singing, or feel the wind blowing. If you are close to the sea, make sure to watch the water, lapping across the pebbles on the shore, and observe the trees swaying in the wind. See the breathtaking sunrise and sunset, notice how in minutes a blanket of darkness overcomes light and how the light wins over darkness, and there in its full glory is the moon. See the stars shining like bright torches in complete darkness. Always do what comes naturally to you; there is no right or wrong way to enjoy your natural environment.

When you give permission for nature to play a much larger role in your daily life, you authorise it to become your natural stress reducer. That is the true power of nature, particularly, when your life seems out of balance, and you continue to explore all it has to offer. You've begun to understand how to fully appreciate the serenity of your environment. When you observe nature, rarely will you encounter the same experience twice.

Our natural environment is everywhere, and not just in parks, woodlands, forests and mountains. It's in your cities. How many times a day do you come across places that have gardens, trees or even plants? How many times a day do you allow yourself to notice them? During your busy, hectic, stressful life, you may fail to think about anything other than duties and your external work priorities. The next time you are on your mobile phone, or any other device, put it down. Take a moment to tune into nature; it is always calling out … you just need to listen.

Chapter 2

Silence The Voices

In 2005 the National Science Foundation published an article regarding research about human thinking. The average person has between 12,000 and 60,000 thoughts per day. Of those, 80% are negative and 95% are exactly the same repetitive thoughts as the previous day.

The research suggested that the apparent fact that only 20% of our thoughts are recorded as positive indicates that, as human beings, we are hard-wired to think in this way. Therefore, it is important that we recognise this and stop beating ourselves up about our constant negative thoughts. Instead, we have to work extremely hard to change our thought process. Understanding a little more about how our minds work can alleviate a lot of unnecessary anxiety when it comes to learning how to operate differently. I have found that many people have experienced what they call their internal voices constantly giving them ideas and thoughts that they are not fully in control of, and that are not always welcome. These voices can seem to be always present.

If I ever questioned myself or wanted to try something new, I would be flooded with doubt, and my internal voices would start chattering away:

- You can't do that Abi.

- You've never done that before Abi.
- What makes you think that you can actually do that and be successful?
- You have no experience in that area.
- You need a certificate before you can do it.
- Stick to what you know, at least you know what you know and it's safe.

These voices would go around and around in my head, like a merry-go-round. But I had another voice, albeit small, fighting hard to be heard, that would be saying

You should really give this a try; you don't know what you're capable of until you *actually do it.*

I know you might be feeling scared; it's only because it's something new; don't discount it until you've done it.

I decided it was time for me to silence those voices that were not in support of what I wanted to do. Over time I created practical ways of minimising them, until I got to the point where the little voice that was always so quiet and reserved became the louder voice, and helped to reduce much of the negative chatter that was constantly taking over my thoughts.

I'm not saying this is easy. In fact, it's just the opposite. It's not something that comes naturally because, as I've already pointed out, as human beings we are more inclined to concentrate on all the negative thoughts than we do on any positive changes we may have in mind.

However, this is not to say that we cannot make those changes when we want to. My advice to you, based on my own experience as well as many of my clients, is to focus on a positive thought to help you. It doesn't matter how small that might be.

For example, I might wake up in the morning feeling like I didn't really sleep at all the night before. Normally I would say to myself, "I feel so tired, I could just roll back up in a ball and get back into bed." I noticed that, as I was telling myself this, my subconscious mind was finding this memory, the memory of feeling tired. Inevitably I began to feel more tired.

I started focusing on the words that I was using, and instead I began to say "I feel like I need more energy today. If I had more energy I wouldn't feel tired, in fact I'd be up and out of this bed I'm really looking forward to my day!"

Now that may sound strange, but in order to feel more energy, my subconscious mind goes back into what I call my hard drive (this is where your long-term memory is stored) and finds a memory that's related to energy, and I would really start to feel better. I can testify to the fact that, with practice, this really works, and it can be a first step towards changing your life in more fundamental ways.

The more you express positive thoughts the more you are inviting those thoughts to become your reality, and those positive voices will continue to get louder. Think about the best way for you to silence your negative voices or reduce them to a whisper. You may want to meditate and imagine yourself in that new position, imagining your new open plan office and hearing your colleagues congratulating you on your achievement. You may have to work at this, but when you allow yourself to accept positive thoughts and positive suggestions naturally, those negative thoughts and emotions will reduce and become quieter in your mind until they're just a whisper.

Living In Your Freezer

A few years ago, my children introduced me to the term brain freeze. When they spoke about it, invariably it was in relation to something that they had eaten that was extremely cold and sometimes gave them a feeling of brief head tension. My creative mind came up with a different theory. When I sat down and thought about brain freeze, my interpretation meant ruminating thoughts, being frozen in the time and space that you were currently at, too afraid to look back and too scared to move forward. Always standing still, stuck in the middle with what seemed like, at the time, nowhere else to go. This is what I mean by living in your freezer when we are frozen in our own state of mind; I repeatedly preserved the same thought process. I have had many experiences of living in my own freezer. Backwards and forwards, the same thoughts, too afraid to take that next step; even though I knew deep down the next step would help me to move on from my current state of mind.

I started to recognise that the safe space that I thought I constantly needed to be in was holding me back. It no longer served its purpose, and I needed to feel confident with the thawing out process. What I mean by that is allowing my emotions and feelings to expand outward. This was not always pleasant; going through significant changes can be quite daunting. However, I know from experience that it can also be extremely liberating.

I wanted to understand why I was stuck in this state, so I decided to start keeping a journal. The best time of day for me was early in the morning. I wrote it in my own handwriting, instead of typing it on the computer, and I found doing it this way was very therapeutic for me. There was nothing complex about my writings; I wrote about my fears and worries, and also about my aspirations and the changes I wanted to create. I questioned my thoughts in writing, and wrote down what I was doing to myself that was holding me back and helping me to stay almost frozen in time. It was so much easier for me to answer my own thoughts when they were out of my head and down on paper; I could clearly see how irrational some of them were, which was far more challenging when those thoughts were in my mind. I also used my journal time to write about the fun things that I wanted to incorporate during my day.

Are you still living in your freezer? Do you recognise that some of your thoughts are way past their sell-by date, the ice crystals are getting thicker and thicker and have no intention of thawing out anytime soon? Sometimes the best that you can do is stop playing safe. Life continues, and every day is a new day that gives you the opportunity to start fresh all over again.

Create your own way of managing your thought process. A journal may not work for you; it could be reading, drawing, or something else that is of interest to you. This may be a gradual process for you, and so what? This is about you and your life; it's not about other people and how quickly they seem to be making changes. This is about you, so concentrate on you and YOU WILL begin to make those necessary changes in your life.

The Importance Of Quiet Time

Have you ever woken up in the morning and suddenly your mind becomes full of tasks that you need to do during the day, and before you even get out of bed it all seems too much, until you feel yourself becoming overwhelmed?

I know that I have felt this way many times, when all I want to do is curl up in a ball and pull the duvet over my head. I'm sure you will agree this is not the greatest way to start your new day. So now, every day, I sit and carry out this 10-minute exercise:

Think about all the goodness that you have in your life right now and remember to focus on how abundant the day ahead is going to be for you. If you have your own daily mantra, or you wish to create one that is being kind to yourself and others then go ahead and say it out loud. I have listed three simple affirmations below; feel free to use any of those to begin with until you are ready to create what is right for you. This is only a 10-minute exercise, so it is short enough that you can complete it every day. Keep a record of your days of abundance. This is a great way to start creating just what you want in your life.

"I forgive myself for being so unforgiving of myself."
"I am open to what life has to teach me."
"I'm happy and healthy every day in every way."

Being quiet and alone first thing in the morning can add great value to the day ahead. It can allow issues to surface that you may spend energy holding at bay, and offer an opportunity to clarify thoughts, hopes, dreams and desires. It provides time and space for you to step back for a short time and evaluate your life. Spending time this way prepares you to re-engage with your relationships and busy work schedule.

Heartfelt Intuition

For many years I thought that I listened to my own intuition; I now know that I wasn't listening at all, and as I reached my late 30s, early 40s, I was really struggling to feel satisfied in many areas of my life. I separated from my partner of 10 years during my 39th year, and this seemed life-shattering for me at that time. You may have had your own similar experiences. I vividly recall at this time of my life, there were days when I felt totally alone, abandoned, with very low self-confidence, and almost as though I had lost my own purpose. I questioned whether indeed I had a purpose and if I ever did. I absolutely love my children and they both helped me through these challenging times. My daughter was only 8 years old, but she would sense that I was unhappy and offer to make me tomato soup or a sandwich, and tell me it would be okay. My son was only five, so he didn't fully understand what was happening around him, but in the short term that also helped me.

I was in a senior position at my organisation, which was a not-for-profit company, that helped hundreds of adults and young people gain qualifications and secure long-term employment. I was responsible for 150 staff members, and after 17 years my career had become my life.

Looking back, I morphed into my job title. However, as my life began to unravel before me, I felt that I had to keep up appearances. I could not bring my true feelings to the workplace, and I really struggled every day to keep it together. In fact, there were many days when I felt so low that I would sit in my car outside of my office, wondering who I was and what I was really doing there. Was I even worthy of being there anymore? Those were certainly challenging times for me.

Due to my position, I felt fearful and believed that I was unable to tell anybody about my situation. I eventually confided in one of my directors and I felt such relief after doing this. If this is you right now, find someone in your organisation that you can confide in. I know that my work certainly suffered, and it was noticed, so don't dwell in your emotional turmoil alone.

The feeling of who am I? didn't disappear; the logical thoughts flowing through my left brain were being overridden by my creative right brain, and a burning sensation of knowing what my purpose was and what I was here to do in this world. These thoughts continued to expand. It was similar to listening to the radio in my car, as I would travel home every day, but the narrative was constantly in my mind. I knew in my heart that I no longer wanted to continue with my current career. I slowly, with resistance, started to connect to my soul voice. This is what I had chosen to call my intuition. I started to question my soul mind, which I had chosen to call my subconscious mind, and allow my heart to speak to me. I recognised that the constant stomach pain that I suffered was part of a new-found anxiety, which I had manifested since I was not allowing my true self to shine.

Connecting Your Soul Dots

I had been my own soul imposter for a long time, and by that I mean pretending to be someone who was not my authentic self. I truly disbelieved that I was this person who had the ability to follow my own dreams; I felt all I would ever do was work for somebody else and for that I should be grateful. I never had the confidence to present myself to the world and be accepted for who I was. I had been in a career with the same company for 17 years, which was a very long time, even though I didn't want to admit this to myself at the time. I was struggling to sleep well at night; I would lie awake constantly worrying about work the next day, and whether I would be able to solve the problems. Would I be able to keep it all together without anybody realising that I was going through my own emotional trauma?

You may recognise my thought process, you may have experienced something similar yourself and you may resonate with the words that I am using. I remember feeling that I no longer wanted to experience any further emotional turbulence.

I didn't want to feel the way I was; I just wanted these feelings to disappear, so that everything would be okay, and life could go back to normal. This is very rarely the case. What I had not recognised were all of the lessons that were now manifesting.

These were lessons that I needed to learn. The only way to learn your true life path lessons is to be in that moment and fully experience it, no matter how painful it may seem at the time. Looking back, I can see that this was the beginning of my time of transition, the beginning of my journey into who I was becoming. It was time to remove the armour that I had worn for so many years, it was time to let the barriers down and accept my vulnerabilities. Believe me when I say that this was not done light-heartedly; it took time, energy and concentration on my part. Because I had been my own soul imposter for so long, there were many layers to unravel.

I'd gotten so used to rushing through my life, working from early morning to late at night 6 days a week, almost on autopilot, and that's because subconsciously I was telling myself I didn't want to slow down, I didn't want to look back, I didn't want to question what I was doing with my life.

However, the universe had other plans for me. I gradually started to reflect on my life, and my current circumstances. Then the realisation came to me in that I was the only one that could change my thoughts, change my path and ultimately change my life. I created the term "soul dots." This was my interpretation of experiencing a series of profound moments in my life. It may have been in the form of a conversation with a complete stranger, which helped me to ascertain that I was on the right track. The life changes I was about to embark on were required in order for me to move forward with my new life creations. One of my soul dots was the compelling intuitive feelings that I felt when I would read a personal development book, and a specific chapter seemed like it was written just for me. Another of my soul dots was the emotional turmoil that I underwent when it was time to sever a relationship that no longer served my wellbeing. Each of these was a poignant time in my life that I needed to accept and embrace, as part of my own transformation. When your soul dots start to magnify between your mind, body and soul, this is your natural inner voice, your intuition which will continue to give you messages. I chose to ignore those messages for many years. I believe that they rarely disappear, and those messages continue to magnify until you are ready to listen and embrace your inner voice.

Only you can assist your soul dots to unite and start a journey with your higher self-connection. Now, you will begin to recognise your true transition and transformation. On the next page, see if you can create a picture or a diagram, and merge your own soul dots. They may look somewhat abstract right now, but that's okay. Find a quiet space to reflect, and think about your journey thus far, your landmarks in your life. Become your own artist and begin to connect your mind, body, soul dot connection. I have purposely been non-descriptive as you may wish to create your own style of soul dots, whatever looks right for you.

Connect Your Soul Dots, Create Your Own Piece Of Art

Chapter 3

Become Aware Of Your Surroundings

When I reflect on my past, there have been times that I spent living in a bubble. What I mean by that is I was so focused on what I thought required action that I missed out on the joy of everyday life that was happening around me. I was very unobservant; I had to re-learn the skill of becoming an observer rather than a task follower. This for me was very much about being present in the moment and observing other people by slowing down my own actions. I made a conscious effort to become the observer. There was a lady called Penny, whom I saw every day but I hadn't really noticed anything about her. I started to observe what she was wearing, what she was reading, her body language when she sat at the bus stop, and I decided to engage with her in conversation. I admit this felt strange at first and a little uncomfortable to me, as we had never spoken.

However, each day the conversation flourished and flowed. We shared many of our everyday life experiences, and each morning it became a joy to meet and engage with Penny at the bus stop.

I thought more about observing people's facial expressions. Are you aware that most communication is non-verbal? I remember being on holiday in Tunisia, about 10 years ago. I was there on my own, and I met a German lady who spoke English and a Russian lady, Svetlana, who spoke no English. On the final night, Svetlana and I decided to go out to eat. I did not speak

Russian and Svetlana did not speak English, yet we communicated through non-verbal body language, and it was incredibly powerful. It really opened my eyes to the importance of understanding universal body language.

You may not be a fan of observing people. Why not observe nature? I never get tired of observing nature: the two birds that land simultaneously on the branch of a tree and sit there chirping, engrossed in their own conversation. The cat that pushes out its claws ready to jump on its prey, the dog that wags its tail waiting for its owner to throw the ball over the other side of the park, the bumblebee feeding on pollen in the heart of the flower. This is the power of observation; you have no choice but to be in the present. This may feel awkward to you as you embark on this new process. What you are really doing is reprogramming your thought process, which over time can only be of benefit to you.

Get Clear On What Really Matters In Your Life

For me, staying focused on a subject was not an easy task. Many times, my mind felt like it was on a rollercoaster ride. Certain thoughts would feel as if they were running at top speed through my mind, and then I would briefly experience a sense of calm, and the same thought process would start again. I don't think I'm the only one who has had this experience. I know how important it is for me to get clear on what really matters in my life, and what I really want. I've learnt how to calm down my thought process and ignore many of my common thought interruptions. These are the very things that I allow my attention to drift towards. For instance, I know that leaving my mobile phone outside the office, or switching it off, will be a great help to me in terms of getting focused and completing the task at hand.

If you know you cannot resist being distracted by every sound alert that your phone or device creates, or if you have the television playing in the background on your favourite TV programme, then switch it off. This is already a familiar distraction that is not going to allow you to give your full attention to what really matters. Start planning how you want your day to be from the night before. It is best to do this with a clear head. For a few moments before you go to sleep, visualise the day that lies ahead of you, and how successful it's going to be. To help you create your vision, begin by thinking about and identifying your own core values, what your passions are, what drives you, what you truly believe in. How can you make a difference in this world? Be as specific as you can and remember to be clear. Your vision may only start with what you want for tomorrow, but as you grow and develop your technique, your vision will grow and develop further, and your creations may become more concise. The key is to have an initial idea, so you know why you're doing what you're doing, and that in turn gives you the opportunity to feel more satisfied and happier whilst you're doing it.

Your vision will not stay static. You may find, as you grow and develop, that your vision grows and develops with you. It is fluid and it is changeable. Your imagination never stands still. Let your creative side flow and see what it is you really wish to achieve. You may prefer specific clear goals, and there's absolutely nothing wrong with that. Goals can be a great stepping stone, building mini bridges to your ever-growing vision; it's also easy to become consumed by the detail and lose the visionary picture you have created for yourself, so just be mindful of this as you are building your vision.

Many people enjoy making a vision board. You can cut out pictures from magazines, use printouts from the internet, or take photos of nature, your favourite food, herbs, plants, etc.;

anything that resonates with you and the life you are creating. Place them on your vision board and build a story around the visual representation. If this works for you then start here. There is no right or wrong way to do this; it's what feels right for you as this is what matters in your life.

Do Something Different Today

Have you ever woken up in the morning, knowing that you were preparing for the same daily experience that occurs every day? It's like your life is stuck in a rut. I have been there, and it was not the best place to be. My life had become so monotonous and routine that I almost forgot how to enjoy myself, to let my hair down and have fun. How was it that I had swiftly gone from living an exciting fun-filled life, to very little pleasure at all? I came to the realisation that it was no longer a natural extension of me. Somehow, I had allowed the mundane and monotonous to become my normality. The funny thing is I remember in my early 20s, telling myself that I would never be this person; I would always be the life and soul of the party, always the last woman standing. Well, I certainly didn't live up to my own expectations. It was time for a change. I met up with a very good friend of mine, and we were reminiscing about all the fun we used to have back in the day, and frankly I'd forgotten about a lot of it. We said our goodbyes, and I went back to my daily dose of boringness.

I decided for the next month I was going to search online, find and then join a natural health Meetup group. I research some events, booked myself onto a self-development seminar, checked out music venues and the genre that I enjoyed, and attended a vegetarian food festival. I was amazed at how many local events were free of charge. The point is that I wanted to make a change to liven up my life, to meet new people and understand that life is always about balance. There will always be more work to do; the phrase "There are not enough hours in the day" is true. When you embrace the areas in your life that make you smile, these are memories that you and your new-found friends will learn to cherish, when you look back on these events in the future. If you think more about creating happy heartfelt memories, you have no choice but to be happier in your endeavours. Whatever you do that is different today, tomorrow or the following day is the right decision for you; it is so easy to talk yourself out of anything different, or anything that feels outside of your comfort zone. Just remember when you dedicate a few hours to your own self-empowerment, everybody benefits from you becoming an improved version of yourself.

Here are a few ideas to get you started; choose which ones resonate with you:

- Get out of bed 10 minutes earlier.
- Try something new for breakfast.
- Walk a different way to the bus stop or drive a different route to work
- Be the host, arrange to entertain your close friends or family invite them out for dinner.
- Rearrange your furniture, change the layout of your bedroom or front room.
- Repaint an area that is in need of redecoration
- Go dancing - join a dance club either near home or on your way home from work, meet some new people and learn how to dance to something new.
- Join an adult education class, photography, theatre, music and language. You will meet new people who share your interests which is where you want to be.
- Plan a weekend away - jump on a train or a coach and explore a new city, this doesn't have to be expensive, you

can do this very reasonably and what a great sense of achievement you will have when you return.

Barefoot Breathing

How often have you thought to yourself, I would love to go outside, kick my shoes off and walk barefoot on the grass; it seems so relaxing? I would like to share with you why it not only seems so relaxing, it may also help improve your health and wellbeing. I love walking on the grass barefoot. As soon as I take my shoes off and my feet are connected with my natural environment, I experience a calming, relaxing and grounding feeling. What I've recently discovered, which has really excited me, explains why I feel the way I do when I'm walking barefoot on the grass. This work has been carried out extensively by Clinton Ober, and it's called Earthing.

Throughout history, our ancestors have sat, walked, and slept on the ground without even knowing that such simple contact transfers a natural electrical signal to the body. It's only in recent years, through the work of Clinton Ober and colleagues, that we are now learning that the earth's electrical energy maintains the order of her own bodily frequencies. Most people are totally unaware of their bioelectrical nature; very few people have any idea that there is an electrical or energetic connection between our bodies and that of the earth. Therefore, many people are unaware of how disconnected they have become from the Earth, and that's due to the creation of shoes, insulating synthetic soled shoes. The shoes still connect with the earth, but as energy frequency humans, we no longer connect. Think about this: both of your feet, with so many nerve endings, very rarely touch the ground anymore; in fact you are far more likely to cover up your feet even on the beach.

Mother Earth can surely help to keep us healthy inside and out; natural frequencies of the earth release electrons that work in a similar way to antioxidants. When you have better contact with the earth, you're actually grounded; you are allowing your body to naturally receive and become charged with these electrons. This in turn helps to reduce electrical imbalances in the body, which reduces the free radicals involved in chronic inflammation and many other diseases, and restoring the body's natural electrical state. I was so excited when I read about this, I immediately went outside, took off my shoes and walked around my garden. The following day I did the same in the woodlands nearby, and I felt totally connected to the earth. If you have a garden, or you live near a park or an open green space, take off your shoes and try this experience for yourself. It works best if you can spare between 5 to 20 minutes. The longer you do it the better your body will respond. I incorporate the Earthing technique along with my pure therapeutic grade essential oils which are all gifts from the earth. I believe this gives me a much stronger foundation of health and a heightened feeling of well-being, which is why I believe I am rarely unwell. This is one of the easiest things in the world to do, and if you're unable to do it with your feet, then do it with your hands or any other part of your body. The key is being in direct contact with the earth, and you will truly benefit from this experience. I'm confident that you will enjoy this. Don't forget to spread the word.

A Sense Of Connection

When I reflect on my range of experiences so far, and how I choose to balance my emotional health, physical health, nutrition, water intake, and barefoot walking, I feel a much greater sense of connection to the earth and to Mother Nature. I sense that I'm constantly moving one step closer to nature.

Whilst I don't pretend to have a detailed understanding of nature and all her complexities, I feel so much more tuned in to the planet that surrounds me, even if it's only a piece of it that I experience each day. There are times when I stand outside our house and look up into the sky, just as the sun is glowing bright orange and red; almost replicating a ball of fire. Within a few mesmerising minutes, the sun has disappeared and been absorbed into the skyline. I watch in admiration. There are no words for when nature truly touches your spirit; the most that you can do is observe, and smile. I am always thankful that I have experienced the opportunity in the first place.

Do you feel closer to nature? What have you seen? What would you like to see? Do you feel that you are growing empathetically? Are you starting to demonstrate more patience with people in your life? Are you feeling less stressed about many of your daily tasks? Have you managed to make time to reconnect by walking through parks, woodlands, forests, and feel the presence of the trees? For many of us, this is very grounding.

After all trees, plants and shrubs produce around 50% of the oxygen that we inhale 365 days a year. A tree that's 100 years old in tree years is just a small child, as there are many trees that are over 2,000 years old, still helping us to stay alive.

When you experience your newly found sense of connection, you may find that some of your old ideas and habits will change rapidly, in a positive way; your eyes are looking at the world through a new pair of lenses. Remember when you are connecting to the world of nature, you also need to disconnect from the incoming mobile phone calls, and all other forms of media; otherwise you will continue unwittingly to see the world through somebody else's eyes.

You may not have even thought about this up until now, and that's why I'm asking you the questions; connection is also about new relationships with one another. It's often a kind word offered to a stranger. It may be somebody that has no home to go to that night, and just by you acknowledging, instead of ignoring the individual, this may help improve both your outlook on the day ahead, and theirs.

Take some time to reflect on your new positive experiences; you may only be at the beginning of your journey, which means it can only get better from now on.

Chapter 4

What Are Essential Oils?

The Three Most Commonly Used Essential Oils

Before I start sharing the benefits of 100% pure essential oils, I want to explain what they are. Essential oils are natural aromatic compounds produced by plants. The oil can be found in various parts of the plants, including the rind, seeds, roots, leaves, flowers, and bark. If you ever inhaled the aroma of fresh mint leaves, you have experienced the aromatic properties of essential oils.

These natural compounds help the plant adapt to its ever-changing environment, protecting against external threats, whilst constantly strengthening its own immune system. Essential oils are the immune system of plants, which is why they have powerful benefits for us. When they are correctly extracted from the plant, without any additional ingredients, they are non-toxic and without side effects.

It's important to educate yourself on using essential oils safely and appropriately, just as you would any other form of complementary medicine. There are three ways that you can benefit from using an essential oil:

Topical use - the essential oil is applied directly to the skin. Essential oils are fat soluble, and the chemical compounds are readily absorbed and enter the bloodstream. It's important to test for any skin sensitivities, and you should always use a high-quality carrier oil such as an organic coconut oil or extra virgin olive oil. Carrier oils do what their name suggests; they" carry" essential oils onto the skin for absorption. This also slows down the rate of evaporation.

Aromatic use - inhalation of an essential oil supports many body systems, including the respiratory and nervous systems. This method uses our sense of smell. Aromatic use of essential oils has the power to influence mood very quickly. Our sense of smell is very closely connected to regions of the brain that control our long-term memory, emotions and hormones. Oils can be diffused into the air using an oil diffuser, inhaled directly from the bottle, or applied to jewellery and clothing. Do not heat essential oils as this will alter their chemistry.

Internal use - essential oils should only be taken internally when they have been thoroughly tested, to ensure there are no impurities or chemicals added to the oil. We consume aromatic compounds naturally as part of our diet in everyday foods. Many essential oils can be consumed internally by adding them to foods or beverages, or in a vegetable capsule. Essential oils are more potent than the whole plant; therefore, small amounts should be used when taking oils internally. Not all essential oils are appropriate for internal use. These include oils from the needles of trees such as pine essential oil and some bark essential oils. Always use a glass or stainless-steel bottle instead of any synthetic material; this will ensure that there are no toxins released into your fluid whilst you are ingesting the essential oils.

Essential Oil Safety Guidelines

As always it's important to be aware, understand and follow the appropriate guidelines, which I have outlined below.

- Do not apply essential oils directly to your eyes, ear canals, nose or an open wound.
- Keep out of reach of children and animals.
- Prior to using an essential oil, consult your doctor or health professional, particularly if you are pregnant, or nursing, or have a pre-existing health condition.
- The use of a carrier oil is recommended as this will help to improve absorption. For children, or those with a skin sensitivity, always dilute with a good carrier oil.
- If you manage to apply an essential oil to an area of sensitivity such as, eyes, ears or nose, refrain from using water. Always wash away with another carrier oil, as water may intensify the effect.
- Citrus essential oils can cause photosensitivity when used topically. Avoid sun exposure for up to 12 hours after application.
- Essential oils that are termed "hot" (meaning they are more likely to cause skin irritation, rather than a heat- based sensation) should always be diluted. This could include oils such as oregano, cassia, birch, cinnamon, clove, eucalyptus, ginger, lemongrass, peppermint, thyme and wintergreen.
- Remember that children are more sensitive than adults, and therefore smaller amounts of oil are more appropriate.
- If you have a pet, and you diffuse an oil, ensure your pet is able to leave the room if it chooses to.
- Consider carrying out a skin test before using an essential oil for the first time. This is important if you have a skin sensitivity or another known allergy.

- Store essential oils in a cool dark place, away from direct sunlight.
- Essential oils are the most potent part of the plant; therefore, just as you would use any other form of complimentary medicine, ensure that you use with care and respect. Remember small amounts used more frequently are more powerful than infrequent large amounts of essential oil.
- Finally, some traditional essential oil users state that internal use of essential oils is not safe. However, there is so much modern research about internal use, by hundreds of thousands of users over many years, that indicates that internal use following appropriate and safety guidelines is perfectly safe. Remember to complete your own research and find a good quality brand that will suit you and your family's requirements. Enjoy your essential oil experience.

The Purity And Potency Of Essential Oils

I must share with you this important information; not all essential oils are made equal. What I mean by that is you only need a small percentage of essential oil in a bottle and it is perfectly legal in many countries to label it as 100% pure essential oil. This is because the bottle may be mixed with a carrier oil; therefore it is 100% pure oil, but not the active compound from the essential oil.

Therefore, I only use and discuss dōTERRA essential oils, because I'm confident that they are tested extensively for their purity and potency, and are certified to be free of pesticides, herbicides and any other chemical residues. When you are using essential oils and many other natural health products, remember to check the small print and ensure that they are 100% natural. As well as using them aromatically, and topically, due to the testing process that dōTERRA employs, you can ingest many of dōTERRA's essential oils using a vegetable capsule. To gain a better understanding, carry out your own research, and decide which essential oils meet your needs. It's important that there are no pesticides, fillers or other synthetic substances found in the essential oils that you choose to use, as you will absorb those chemicals into your body.

If you decide to use an essential oil aromatically, you may wish to place a few drops into a diffuser. This is a much better option than using an oil burner. When you heat up an essential oil, by using a candle at the bottom of an oil burner, with a small amount of water above the candle, you will reduce any of the therapeutic benefit of the oil. This is due to essential oils being volatile, which means they will evaporate with heat. If the essential oil has been mixed with a synthetic perfume, then you may be releasing toxins into the air, that you will directly inhale into your blood stream, and these are consequently carried throughout the cells in your body.

This mechanism does not heat up the oil; it operates through ultrasound. You add water and it releases steam from the top of the diffuser. Inhaling the pure essential oils will be of great therapeutic benefit to you and your family.

Whilst I am talking about toxins, do you have any idea of how many different chemicals you may have in your home? I'm talking about cleaning products, in your kitchen, in your bathroom, in your lavatory. Look at how many products tell you that you are using a controlled substance hazardous to health (COSHH). You are inhaling these toxic fumes every time you clean your bathroom and other areas in your home.

If you are unaware, as I was for a very long time, take some time to read the labels on many of your household products that you purchase, whilst carrying out your weekly shop in the supermarket.

Let's talk about a chemical called sodium laureate sulphate or sodium lauryl sulphate (SLS); they're actually the same thing and can be very harmful. Studies show that it has been linked to organ toxicity, skin irritation and endocrine disruption. *SLS*, as it is called for short, is a synthetic chemical that is used in many of our everyday household products, such as toothpaste, body wash, soap, shampoo, conditioner, makeup and hand sanitizer. It is also used to clean garage floors; it is an engine degreaser and is used for industrial strength soaps. All of these products are synthetic, and have tried to mimic plant-based surfactants that we find in nature. This is why there may be specific side effects affiliated with many of these products that you may use every day; totally unaware of how your internal organs are responding to the chemicals. Any further research that you may choose to do will provide you with more awareness of these potential side effects.

Lemon, Lavender And Peppermint

Lemon essential oil has been used for its therapeutic benefits for over 1000 years. Its healing benefits are well documented, and there are many scientific studies that have been carried out on lemon essential oil; it not only smells wonderful it is also multifaceted.

You may have tried squeezing lemon juice into your water. I did this for many years; it is a very common practice for people to start their daily cleansing routine, usually first thing in the morning. However, were you aware that the flesh of the lemon is very acidic and therefore may remove the enamel from your teeth? Have you ever been to the dentist and (s)he may have asked you if you have been squeezing lemon into your water? This might be the reason why your teeth have been affected, so just be aware of this in the future.

When you use lemon certified therapeutic grade essential oil, the lemon oil is from the rind of the fruit; therefore it is alkaline and not acidic. If you decide to put 1 drop into your glass of water it will not affect your teeth, and is a highly effective detoxifier.

Here are some of the top uses for lemon essential oil:

- Detoxifying your body
- Breaking down congestion and mucus
- Stem varicose veins
- Stress reduction
- Promoting weight loss
- Heartburn and acid reflux reduction
- Cutting through grease and grime
- Use it as a furniture polish
- Effective as a kitchen surface cleaner
- Removing bad odours

One of my morning rituals is to put 1 drop of lemon essential oil in my glass of water as soon as I rise. This is the best time of the day to cleanse toxins out of my body, so if you wish to incorporate lemon essential oil into your body cleansing routine, it's a great way to start your day.

Lemon essential oil on an emotional level is also very uplifting, invigorating and refreshing. Ensure as a safety measure to avoid exposure to sunlight or UV rays for 12 hours after direct application to your body, as it may cause skin sensitivity.

Lavender essential oil is one of the most versatile essential oils that I'm familiar with. If another person were to mention lavender essential oil to you, would you recognise it as an oil that you have used previously? If so let me take a guess at what you may have used it for.

Lavender is well-known for all things calming and healing. Lavender is one of the most studied essential oils that exist today. Most people use lavender to help them sleep. It's associated as calming to the body and it's a natural sedative. It's very relaxing and soothing. It's also antibacterial, antispasmodic and regenerative. Not only is lavender good for helping you to sleep, it is incredible for burns and scarring. Let me give you an example. When I'm rushing around in my kitchen cooking for my children, who rarely put the oven gloves back in the drawer where they belong, I generally use a tea towel when taking things out of the oven, and I've burnt my hand on the metal oven tray. I just reach for my bottle of lavender which I keep in my kitchen, and put 1 to 2 drops around the burn. It significantly reduces the stinging sensation, and effectively cleanses the wound and encourages faster healing.

If you are new to the world of essential oils, lavender is a great starting point. Lavender is the most commonly used essential oil in the world today, and it is widely used in aromatherapy and in the perfumery industry. The scent has a calming effect which aids in relaxation and the reduction of stress and anxiety. It also has antiseptic and analgesic properties, which as I've mentioned will ease the pain of a burn, prevent infection and promotes rapid healing. It can be used with massage oils to effectively relieve joint and muscle pain, and it is also a powerful antioxidant; it is highly antimicrobial and is a natural antidepressant. There are so many benefits to the use of this incredible essential oil.

"In 1910 French chemist and scholar René-Maurice Gattefossé discovered the virtues of the essential oil of lavender. Gattefossé badly burned his hand during an experiment in a perfumery plant and plunged his hand into the nearest tub of liquid, which just happened to be lavender essential oil.

I want to share something with you about lavender and its history. Did you know that lavender was used by the Egyptians? Only the royal family were granted use of this powerful essential oil; it was used for embalming, massage and creating cosmetics. This was over 2000 years ago.

Lavender has so many healing benefits, some of which I have listed below:

* Helps to improve sleep
* Reduces stress and anxiety
* Effective for improving focus and concentration
* Incredible for burns and mosquito bites
* Supports migraines and headaches
* Effective on sensitive and dry skin

When I am travelling to either Europe or other parts of the world for a public speaking event, I find it challenging to sleep somewhere unfamiliar on my first night. Therefore, I always carry a bottle of lavender with me; I rub it on the soles of my feet before I go to bed, and that ensures that, wherever I am in the world, I experience a good night's sleep.

Lavender is also very effective for migraines and headaches. You can either inhale it or apply topically on your temples and on the back of your neck. Always be aware that if you have any kind of skin sensitivity you must always use a carrier oil to mix with the lavender.

Peppermint essential oil: Many people have been introduced to peppermint, primarily in the form of a cup of tea. I was introduced to peppermint essential oil over 20 years ago and whilst I recognise that it wasn't as pure as the dōTERRA essential oil, it did instantly clear my nasal passage, and was exceptionally powerful as I suffered regularly from colds in my younger years.

Peppermint essential oil has the ability to speedily expand your airways. Just a reminder that I am discussing 100% pure certified therapeutic grade oils, which are 50 to 70 times stronger than herbs. This is why one drop of pure peppermint is equivalent to over 20 cups of peppermint tea; so if you are a peppermint tea lover, this is a great essential oil for you to either inhale or diffuse. Peppermint is another oil that is very commonly known around the world; it has been used for hundreds of years. I love using peppermint in my diffuser first thing in the morning; it's effective for getting the family moving, and it not only helps clear all our airways; it's very helpful for focus and concentration.

I regularly drive long distances to either teach classes or as a guest speaker at a natural health event. I rarely leave home without my bottle of peppermint. I rub one drop on my chest and one drop across the back of my neck. Peppermint is highly effective for long distance driving; whilst I'm always safe and drive within my limits, it helps to keep me alert and awake as well as keeping my nasal passage clear, and it also smells divine. When we go on family holidays, I use it as a mosquito repellent. Spiders and ants also dislike it.

This oil is highly anti-inflammatory and will help support the reduction of general joint and muscle aches and pains. It's also very stimulating, so if you need an energy boost it's a great oil to either ingest or put a drop in your hand and inhale.

Peppermint can be warming or cooling; it depends on what your body needs to bring it back into balance. If you have a skin sensitivity, you may wish to use it with a carrier oil.

There are many benefits that this oil offers:

- Releasing blocked sinuses
- Improved focus and concentration
- Reducing feelings of nausea
- Effective for burns (use one drop on top of lavender helps to cool the burn)
- Cooling effect within the body
- Reducing stomach cramps
- Helpful for bad breath
- Loss of sense of smell
- Food cravings
- Allergies

Lemon, lavender, and peppermint are all natural antihistamines. If you suffer from any form of seasonal allergies, you may find these three essential oils extremely beneficial. Peppermint is known as an enhancer oil, and therefore will help intensify the benefits of both lavender and lemon.

My son was a severe hay fever sufferer. Many trees begin to pollenate around February, and he would start to sneeze uncontrollably first thing in the morning. His eyes would become very itchy, and the constant sneezing made him feel tired before he arrived at school. This exceptional blend of essential oils helped to reduce his hay fever symptoms. The easiest way for you to use these oils is to purchase a 10ml rollerball bottle. Ensure that it is glass. Fill the rollerball bottle with 50% of a good organic carrier oil. I always use fractionated coconut oil, which is coconut oil with the fat removed. Use one that you are comfortable with, and ensure that it is of good quality. Then add 20 drops of lemon, 20 drops of lavender, and 5 drops of peppermint. Note that this recipe is not exclusive; it's a ratio that I use for my teenage son and my family.

Another effective way to use these essential oils is by putting them into a diffuser. All you need is one drop of each oil. You can diffuse them in the bedroom before your child goes to sleep; this will also help your child gain a good night's sleep, which can be quite a challenge if, due to the allergy, your child's nose is constantly blocked. The same principle works with adults.

Please be aware, if you are pregnant and breastfeeding, that peppermint essential oil will help to reduce lactation, therefore be mindful of using this oil during pregnancy.

Chapter 5

The Power Of Your Emotions

I have always been fascinated by my emotions, and how they interact with my brain and the rest of my body. I've noticed how my emotional response changes when I'm surrounded by different groups of people. For instance, when I'm asked to speak on stage about natural health, I experience excitement and happy emotions leading up to the event, and I always look forward to these events. As the event day approaches and I'm driving to the event, my focus gets fuzzy and unclear, and my stomach starts to rumble even though I'm not hungry. I'm emotionally experiencing mild anxiety; I have learnt to recognise this emotion, and channel all my nervous energy into the subject that I'm passionate about, and use it to enhance my overall performance. However, in my early days of public speaking it wasn't always like this. I didn't know how to harness my emotions, and as I went onstage my mouth would go dry, I found it hard to swallow, and I could hear the strain in my voice. I had to learn how to ground myself and harness my energy to improve my performance, which over time I have managed to enhance.

What are our emotions? The limbic system is an area that is known as the seat of our emotions; this is where you experience fear, anger, sadness, anxiety, and love. It is also part of your subconscious mind, where you store all of your memories. Your emotional brain sorts out all incoming stimuli as either pleasurable or threatening. There is a particular area in the brain which is the size of an almond; it's the detector of our emotional brain and it's called the amygdala; your brain's response to your fight or flight mode. Neurotransmitters such as serotonin and dopamine are used as chemical messengers to send signals across your brain network; different areas of the brain receive these signals, which in turn allow you to recognise specific objects and situations that you encounter. The next step is to assign an emotional value that will help guide your behaviour in terms of how you deal with that specific situation.

Your limbic system fits underneath your cerebrum, which is the largest part of the brain. It is made up of structures such as the hypothalamus, hippocampus, and the little almond-shaped fight or flight area that I've already mentioned is the amygdala.

The purpose of expressing your emotions is to share how you truly feel, to be open and honest, not to feel embarrassed or embarrass another person. There may be times when you need to express your pain or sadness; many of my clients suffer significant feelings of apprehension. Some of my clients express their concerns, and share that once they open up emotionally, and start to speak about their pain or sadness, they are fretful about the inability to suppress further emotional turmoil that may follow. For many individuals these emotions have been stifled for years. Initially, there was a time in your life that triggered those deep-seated emotions. What I would like you to recognise is that, without exploring the root cause, these deep-seated emotions can cause a chemical reaction in your body which may lead to illness and disease. This is why it's so important to express your emotions and your feelings in order to lead a much healthier, balanced life.

How Does The Body Store Emotions?

Perhaps many of us better understand how we experience emotions, but is it true that we really store emotions in the body? And if so, how do we do this? Have you ever felt emotional or even cried unexpectedly, and subsequently asked yourself why the tears were created? Remember that tears enable you to experience an effective form of relief. Many of us hold onto grudges, anger and resentment. Think about how knotted and tight your shoulders become when you are stressed, or how your stomach turns into a roller coaster when you are apprehensive or nervous. You may believe that you have forgiven on an intellectual level. However, your body may not agree with this, and it recognises that your particular emotional response continues to stagnate internally.

Dr Candace Pert was a pioneering neuroscience researcher who, whilst still a graduate student at Johns Hopkins in the late 1970s, discovered the brain opioid receptor. She died in 2013, but not before continuing groundbreaking research into the mind, creating a bridge between traditional science and new age thinking. Dr Candace Pert wrote a phenomenal book, *Molecules of Emotion: The Science Behind Mind Body Medicine*. She was very much a believer in alternative medicine. As a female in the 1970s, she decided to discard the suit and wear clothes that matched her own personality. They were both flowery and colourful, and very much against the grain of the male scientist world at that time.

Psychologists often blame mood disorders on unbalanced neurotransmitters in the brain. Are you aware that your stomach has so many neurons, in fact more than the peripheral nervous system, that some researchers now call it the second brain? The integration of mind and body doesn't stop there. As Pert discovered, the body cannot be discussed as separate from the mind. Our emotions trigger the release of special compounds called peptides that are stored by the body, whether in a tissue organ or muscle. "I think unexpressed emotions are literally lodged in the body," Pert said. The real true emotions that need to be expressed are in the body, trying to move up and be expressed and thereby integrated, made whole and healed. To feel and understand means you have worked it all the way through. Your emotions have risen all the way to the surface. You are integrating at higher and higher levels in the body, bringing your emotions into consciousness. Listed below are five areas in the body where we store specific emotions.

Anger

Anger affects the liver more than any other organ; these are symptoms to look for:

- Headaches
- Itchy skin
- Skin conditions
- Easily irritated
- Low energy

Identify healthy outlets to deal with the stress and emotions of life. Suppressed anger over time may cause internal ailments, and could eventually evolve into depression. Find healthy ways to release it. Seek out nature, scream in the forest or woodlands, let it out. If it feels better for you, shout into your pillow, punch your pillow, write about it and then tear up the pages. Uncover what works best for you.

Grief

Grief is stored in the lungs and when prolonged, can result in:

- Tightness in chest
- Recurring bronchitis
- Asthma
- Pain in the chest shoulder and back
- Cough
- Dry mouth and throat
- Hoarseness
- Weight loss

Talk to a therapist and caring friends. Heavy loads need to be voiced and shared. Write it out, cry it out, allow yourself to "be" with sadness rather than stifling or ignoring it. Giving it time and space will eventually help it dissipate. The time factor is different for each one of us.

Worry

The stomach suffers the long-term effects of worry, weakening digestive fibre. This lowers hydrochloric acid production and may cause bloating, gas, and changes in bowel habits while thinning gut lining. Being aware of the symptoms may help you to increase your level of relaxation.

Stress

Stress can be extremely harmful to your body. It really targets the heart and brain, leading to anxiety disorders, heart palpitations, insomnia, muscle cramps, and brain fcg. Educate yourself on what triggers your response to stress. Learn new methods of breath work (deep breathing is highly effective), create short daily meditations, take up walking, running, jogging, or pilates/yoga to release excess energy. Any activity that reduces stress will help slow down the unproductive circulation of cortisol throughout your body.

Fear

Fear lives in the kidneys and can manifest as chronic adrenal fatigue, with the never-ending tired-but-wired feeling. Frequent urination, urinary tract infections, back pain, and insomnia due to the inability to "let go" of feeling safe. Breathwork is highly effective when in a fear-based state. Being out in nature and observing your surroundings can be very calming. Walk barefoot on the grass, or beach, whilst grounding and visualize yourself releasing your fear.

Essential Oils And Emotions

I have highlighted how important it is to recognise your emotional state, and how it can make you feel about yourself. You are an energetic being; energy is constantly moving around your body. When you suppress your emotions, your energy flow is out of balance. Even though you have decided to bury that emotion, the result of controlling or suppressing your emotional energy might be frustration, anger, depression, or the physical manifestation of pain, control issues or emotional shutdown. This is when self-judgement, low self-esteem and negative thoughts about yourself may begin to manifest. Also, what you may be unaware of, is that suppressing your emotions uses up a huge amount of energy. This may reduce the amount of energy that should be used for other vital body functions, such as your immune system, and for that there may be a price to pay. Negative emotions overwork your spleen, liver and adrenal glands, which the body needs to sustain itself, and this may result in fatigue, auto immune disorders and a lowered feeling of health and well-being.

One of the ways that the amygdala performs its duties is through your sense of smell. It directly affects your olfactory system, and your sense of smell is necessary for survival. It is one of your oldest senses. For most people it is 10,000 times more powerful than the sense of taste. Aromas have a direct and profound effect on the deepest levels of your body systems. When you inhale an essential oil it enters the olfactory system and directly affects the amygdala. Therefore, essential oils have the power to affect your mood. They can be extremely helpful for individuals who wish to release emotional trauma, which as a therapist I have witnessed many times. The oils' ability to attach themselves to past experiences can initiate rapid responses, both physically and emotionally in the brain, and therefore throughout the rest of the body. Inhalation of essential oils is the most effective method to impact the brain.

Outlined below are areas of your body that may be impacted by your emotions.

Feelings of frustration are stored in your liver. You may suffer from constipation or diarrhoea. Use 2-3 drops of Roman chamomile topically or aromatically. This will help you shift from feeling frustrated to purposeful.

If you suffer from depression, which is generally caused by a lack of serotonin, you may be experiencing gut issues. 90% of your serotonin is stored in your gut. Melissa, frankincense and lavender are natural antidepressants - rub 2 drops of each over your solar plexus area and they will help you move from feeling depressed to feeling light-filled.

Are you suffering from guilt or shame? These emotions are held in the area of the heart. Use peppermint and bergamot with a carrier oil in case of skin sensitivity. Use 2-3 drops of each and rub over your heart area. This will help you to feel less inadequate and more worthy.

Embrace Your Sense Of Smell

A previous client came to see me as he suffered from a condition called Anosmia; this condition is created when you have lost your sense of smell either temporarily or permanently. This can be caused by a traumatic experience, and sometimes individuals are born with this condition. For this story, I will call my client John. As a child, John had suffered a traumatic experience, and because of this he lost his sense of smell at age 11. He came to see me as a clinical hypnotherapist to see if there was anything that I could do to help him regain his sense of smell.

John explained that he was now a father, and he had two children — an 18-month-old baby and a 3-year-old. John had never experienced smelling nappies or smelling that newborn baby scent that most other individuals could when they picked up his children. This made him feel very low and sometimes a little depressed.

We worked together in order to identify the root cause. I asked him if he was open to experiencing essential oils, and he replied yes. I gave him a small bottle of peppermint essential oil and asked him to rub one drop on the palm of his hands and inhale. I asked him to do that every two hours; and when he came back to see me two weeks later, he informed me that he had actually started to gain the sense of smell. This wasn't permanent but was life-changing for John in many ways. I feel that sometimes we do not value our sense of smell until it's taken away from us.

It is one of our oldest senses and we must learn to appreciate it. Your sense of smell also acts like a warning system; you can use it to protect you. For instance, if you detected a strong smell of gas, you would immediately be alerted to the sign of danger and act accordingly.

When you smell an essential oil, it links directly to your limbic system, which is your seat of emotion. This is why essential oils work so seamlessly with our emotions, and have the power to elevate our mood.

When I'm feeling very low on energy or if someone has said something to me in jest that I have taken personally, I will open up a bottle of wild orange, or bergamot and sometimes a mix of citrus oils, as they help to reduce stress and elevate mood. I feel so much better within the space of 60 seconds. Why not try this for yourself? Always use a citrus oil that resonates with you. Place 1 to 2 drops in your hand and inhale, and really focus on elevating your thoughts. This experience should help you to lift your mood.

You Are Your Thoughts

I was not always aware of how powerful my thoughts were; for many years I didn't think that they were that important. However, as I grew and learned, and moved through life experiencing my own journey, I not only became aware of the power of my own thoughts; I began to appreciate and acknowledge a deeper understanding that I was creating my own reality. Whether or not you are conscious of this, your mind is always working, and it is always creating based on your thoughts.

Everything that surrounds you and me started with a thought: the chair you are sitting on, the glasses you may be wearing, the plant pot you may be holding, the car you may be driving, the water from the tap. Everything in this world has its own energy force, no matter how small it may be.

I know that my thoughts, both positive and negative, create my reality, just as your thoughts create your own experience. The question is when you set an intention for yourself, do you want it to create a positive or negative outcome? That may sound like a silly question as most people will say that they want their thoughts to create positive outcomes. If you're not aware of your thoughts, how do you know what kind of outcome you are creating for yourself?

For example, when you focus your true intention on something that you like about a person, naturally your thought process will expand, and you will find more things that you like about that individual. When you focus your intentions on something that you dislike about that person, you will tend to find more areas that you dislike. When I genuinely started to think more about where I was focusing my own attention, and I started to play back some of the scenarios from my past where I had suffered a lot of turbulence, chaos, uncertainty and unhappiness, I began to realise and subsequently accept that many of my situations were self-created. That was the moment when my life experiences started to positively change for me. If you are currently surrounded by chaos and confusion, the thoughts in your head are compounding your experience. If, however, you feel like you are in a really good place, and there's happiness, laughter, joy and sharing, you're really feeling that your subconscious mind is manifesting all of your positive experiences, and you are absolutely right. The outcome is solely reliant on your own state of mind. Your thoughts and your mind are such powerful tools; learn how to make them work well for you, so that you become more aware of how to get the best out of any given situation.

I am not saying this is going to be easy. For some people it may take many years of mastery before they feel confident, and positive thoughts become their reality. You may find that it doesn't take you long at all; you may already be in this space and if you are, ensure that you give yourself a well-deserved pat on the back.

Just remember if you don't like what you see around you, you have the power to recreate it. Know that you are the only one that creates your own story; it is not only satisfying but it's also empowering for yourself, as you continue on your journey of life exploration.

Chapter 6

Three Of The Most Common Conditions

You may know someone who suffers from one or more of the conditions listed in the three bullet points below, or you may suffer from one of them yourself:

- Chronic Pain
- Digestive issues
- Sleep disruption

I wanted to focus on these areas, as these are the most talked about at any of my natural health education classes and seminars.

I will be sharing with you my own experience of chronic pain, in this chapter. Each of the above conditions can be detrimental to living your everyday life, and overtime may greatly affect the relationship that you experience with your family and your friends.

Many times, over the past few years, my clients have shared their health concerns with me. What I have found is that a particular client may have started with two prescription tablets for pain relief, which is totally appropriate. As time progressed, however, the side effects of the medication caused further issues, and my client's medication intake was increased from two to six tablets per day. This was a major cause of concern. Let me be clear: I have no issue with western medicine; I truly believe that western medicine and plant-based medicine work synergistically in the body. However, I also believe that it may be just as beneficial for you to explore a natural plant-based alternative that is much gentler with your body in the short and long term.

Natural Health and Pain Management

Endorphins are naturally produced within your body; these are the hormones that are responsible for pain relief. The more endorphins you produce, the less pain you will experience. You might have heard that exercise is a very effective way to release endorphins. However, if you are in constant pain this is going to prove very challenging. Inflammation is the body's way of alerting us to anything that our body considers harmful. Healthy inflammation is necessary for the body to protect itself against further injury.

There are two types of inflammation: acute and chronic. Acute inflammation may be caused by intense physical workouts, coughs and colds, or a sore throat. Chronic inflammation is much more long-term, and would have occurred over a longer period. It may be that the body was unable to heal itself at the initial stage of inflammation. Conditions such as rheumatoid arthritis, osteoporosis, fibromyalgia, autoimmune diseases and asthma fall into this category.

Pain, which is very similar to inflammation, can be mild or severe. Acute pain such as a toothache can be typically intense and short lived; this pain will subside in a fairly short space of time. Chronic pain is ongoing, and can be mild or intense; this pain may manifest as skeletal pain, strained muscles, or it could include a range of internal organs. The feelings manifest themselves as cramping and aching sensations, and sometimes it may be a constant dull stabbing, pinching or even an internal throbbing feeling.

When managing chronic inflammation, it's important to feed your body with the right nutrition to help reduce the inflammation. When possible eat organic foods. I have listed some nutritional ideas below:

- Turmeric, Chia Seeds, Flax Seeds
- Virgin coconut and olive oil.
- Green leafy vegetables, such as spinach, kale, and broccoli.
- Nuts like almonds and walnuts.
- Fatty fish like salmon, mackerel, tuna, and sardines.
- Fruits such as pineapple, blueberries, cherries, and oranges.

Many pure essential oils are anti-inflammatory, analgesic, and very calming to the body. Listed below are the essential oils that I have informed my clients about, who have expressed the need for further support with managing their pain and inflammation:

- Wintergreen - serious aches and pains, warms and supports bone healing
- Peppermint - reduces pain and inflammation, very cooling on your skin
- Helichrysum - reduces pain, accelerates healing, helps reduce toxins
- Black pepper - reduces inflammation; supports pain relief, increases circulation
- Basil - very calming for your nerves, helps to improve circulation

Each of these pure essential oils may be used topically, but always be safe and use with a carrier oil. The one I find most suited to these oils is called fractionated coconut oil, but almond oil or grapeseed oil are also good. It is better if you use an organic oil, or one that has been tested for any impurities. These are just some ideas that you may want to incorporate into your pain management routine, which are natural and free of toxins, and therefore more beneficial to your body.

The Bare Essentials For Pain Relief

When I was pregnant with my second child 15 years ago, I started to suffer from a condition called carpal tunnel syndrome I had no prior knowledge of this condition at the time; I was informed by my doctor that the condition was temporary and would dissipate after the birth of my baby, and life would go back to normal.

However, nothing was farther from the truth. My condition did not disappear; in fact I suffered with CTP for 13 years. For those of you who are unaware of what this condition entails, I will explain:

Carpal tunnel syndrome is a condition in which the median nerve is squeezed when it passes through the wrist. The median nerve controls some of the muscles that move the thumb; it also carries information back to the brain about sensations in your thumb and fingers.

When the nerve is inflamed it is squeezed, causing intense pain or aching, tingling and numbness in the affected hand. Women are more likely than men to develop carpal tunnel syndrome and although the condition affects people of all ages, it's more common in middle-aged and elderly people. My condition emerged at the same time every morning; 4 am like clockwork, I would wake up in excruciating pain up and down my arm, all the way down to my hand. First, I would try and shake it off, but this made my symptoms worse. I would get out of bed, and start pacing up and down the bedroom until the pain subsided, and this could take between 20 minutes and an hour.

I would then go back to bed and try to sleep, but I was wide awake and found it extremely challenging to get back to sleep. I would drive to work early in the morning, and I travelled many miles around the country for work, so when I left home at 6 am, I would sit in my car and wait until my hand regained its normal sensation, and by that I mean its gripping power. I was unable to safely hold on to my steering wheel due to the tingling numb sensation and no gripping power in my hand, and this was very problematic in terms of arriving at work on time.

Three years ago, I was introduced to a blend of essential oils mixed with aloe vera gel called Deep Blue Rub, which was to change my life forever. This blend includes oils such as peppermint, eucalyptus camphor, mentha, and blue tansy, to name a few. All of these are natural anti-inflammatories, and aloe vera is high in antioxidants and is an effective cleansing plant. I used this rub for five and a half weeks and I've been pain free for two and a half years. For me this was an incredible outcome which is why I want to share it with you now; what I'm not saying is that this is a cure or will work in the same way for you. Your internal makeup could be very different to mine so I can only share my own experience. I have received positive feedback from many people who have suffered with chronic pain such as arthritis, osteoporosis and fibromyalgia.

Natural Health And Digestion

What I'm about to say to you might sound strange; are you aware of the three-brain theory? Science has revealed there are processing functions in your mind, heart and gut. The book "mBRAINING" by Grant Soosalu and Marvin Oka explores this theory in great detail. Many years ago, I began to neglect my digestive health. There is a saying that we are what we eat, and it's true. Have you ever used the terminology gut feeling? You may have experienced what many people call butterflies in your stomach. This is not just a coincidence; as mentioned previously, 90% of your body's serotonin is produced in your gut, and this is the hormone that manages your mood. When I was not eating well, I certainly recognised and felt the effects of this. My mood would be erratic, and my energy level was consistently low. I felt tired and lethargic. I had not realised at this stage in my life the importance of my gut health, and how it connected with my brain and my mood.

Our gut bacteria have evolved with us since birth. They help digest our food and fight off unfriendly outsiders like viruses and moulds. To keep us healthy they need to be healthy and plentiful, and when they're not, we feel it.

For those who suffer from anxiety or depression, this is good news: science is telling us that improved diet could have a positive impact on improving your mood. Studies indicate that those with healthy and diverse gut microbes are less likely to suffer from any mood management conditions.

Recently, you've probably heard a lot about probiotics in the news. Probiotics are foods that nourish and promote your biome, which is like your own good bacteria community. They're foods cultured with the strains of healthy bacteria. Yogurt is a great example of a cultured food. Unfortunately, many shop yogurts are little more than a thickened, sweetened milk product. But yogurt that lists strains such as Lactobacillus acidophilus, and Bifidobacterium lactis actually contain the healthy bacteria your gut needs. Are you familiar with the term prebiotic foods? They support a healthy gut ecosystem in which your bacteria can thrive. Together, prebiotic and probiotic foods help keep your second brain full of the right kind of bacteria that your gut needs to fully function.

When we take care of every part of our body, it will naturally take care of us. Many conditions and ailments tend to lead back to poor digestive health. It's important that you are fully aware of what and how you are eating, and the continuous effects that it may have on your overall health. Read on and find out how you can improve your digestive health.

The Bare Essential For Digestive Gut Health

Many years ago, I suffered with my digestive health; mainly mild symptoms such as diarrhoea, constipation and nausea from travel sickness. Now I understand the importance of digestive health and what I eat, how I eat and how much time I give my food to digest is so important. I decided that I needed to change some of my eating habits to support my digestive health. When I am facilitating seminars or classes, I always receive many questions about digestive health issues. I have a growing concern about the number of children that have poor gut health by the age of four or five years old; in my opinion this may be setting them up for more serious health issues as they grow into teenagers and then into adulthood.

I want to share a brief story with you. I was teaching a natural health class and I recall spending a long time answering questions about digestive health issues. A mother approached me and explained that her daughter had suffered with digestive health concerns from the age of two, and she was now aged six. In the last year she had been prescribed antibiotics six times; her daughter was constantly off school, she had missed out on a lot of her education and she constantly had a cold or a cough.

This mother shared with me her concerns about the high amount of antibiotics that her daughter had been prescribed; however, she had no knowledge about anything other than antibiotics. She was unaware of nature's medicine and how it could help restore her daughter's immune system, and therefore was extremely pleased to receive this helpful information.

I'm also asked about detoxifying the gut, a very important process to keep your body healthy and strong. Learning to cleanse your body the right way is straightforward; just remember if it is your first time to go slowly and gently build up your cleanse; you do not want your body to go into full detox symptoms until your body is ready and prepared for this experience.

Below are some other conditions that I am asked about during my classes or seminars, along with the essential oils and natural supplements that may help these conditions:

- Your body needs nutritional support during cleansing and detoxification:
- Life Long Vitality - multi vitamins and minerals, omega fatty acids, support healthy living
- Cleanse and rebuild health gut bacteria
- Increase your water intake, your body needs help flushing out the toxins
- Bentonite clay, effective for clearing the digestive tract
- Probiotics - PB assist, help to build up your good gut bacteria
- Digestive enzymes - Terrazymes - supports the breakdown of undigested food

When possible, increase your intake of organic produce, and drink clean filtered water. You may not always realise how toxic your own home can be. Science has proven that many of the cleaning products that you use in your home are full of chemicals and toxins that you and your family are inhaling every day. Over time these chemicals can be detrimental to your overall health. I understand that this may seem like an added expense at the very beginning of your natural health journey; but it's important to replace the chemicals within your home with natural cleaning products. Also, be aware of your skin regime, your face cream, your skincare, your hair care products, and your deodorant. Is it aluminium free? Each of these chemically laden products may have an impact on your health, so please be aware and read the product information guide. At least you will be aware of what your skin is absorbing, then you can make an informed decision with your replacement products. I have listed below a range of essential oils that will help support digestive health:

- Cilantro - effective for heavy metal elimination
- Lemon and grapefruit- help to reduce fat from your cells
- Geranium - liver detoxification, supports the repair of damaged liver tissue
- Helichrysum - regeneration and detoxification
- Myrrh - scar tissue and inflammation due to disease
- Peppermint- spasms underneath the rib cage
- Digestive blend - gas, burping, nausea, diarrhoea, constipation and vomiting

Always start gradually, and gently build up your dosage with these essential oils. Choose which essential oils are most applicable to your condition and start with small amounts, between 1-2 drops two to three times a day in a vegetable capsule with water. You may wish to use alongside the lifelong vitality multivitamin pack for optimum support.

Natural Health And Sleep

One of the worst experiences that you may have had is being unable to get a good night's sleep. This is such a common problem for so many people. When I used to work in my 9 to 5 job, I would experience many sleepless nights. I would go to bed, my mind full of all the problems that I had to resolve over the next two to three days; I would try and create solutions and become frustrated because I couldn't get to sleep. Just as I was getting to the sleep stage my alarm clock would ring and it was time to get up. On average I was getting around 4 hours sleep per night, which was extremely problematic for me. I struggled to concentrate at work, I would start to feel tired during meetings, and I experienced brain fog and a constant lack of energy.

I imagine that many of you will have experienced a poor night's sleep; now if this is just occurring sporadically or just a one off, then your body will probably adapt accordingly. However, if this is continuous, it may create longer term health concerns.

Sleep is the time when your body ceases to engage in most voluntary functions. This is the time when your body goes into healing mode; it's the perfect time to repair and restore any area that is out of balance.

During this time your conscious brain activity is partially suspended. This is so important and is a key factor in restoring and maintaining your emotional, physical and mental health. Many of my clients who come to see me in a lifestyle coaching capacity, particularly when they are setting up a new business, struggle with their sleeping patterns. One of the most common concerns is insomnia. This is split into categories:

Acute insomnia: A brief episode of difficulty sleeping. Acute insomnia is usually caused by a life event, such as a stressful change in a person's job role, receiving bad news, or maybe a bereavement in the family. Often acute insomnia resolves over a short space of time.

Chronic insomnia: A long-term pattern of difficulty sleeping. Insomnia is usually considered chronic if a person has trouble falling asleep, or staying asleep, at least three nights per week for three months or longer. Some people with chronic insomnia have a long-standing history of difficulty sleeping. Chronic insomnia has many causes.

Sleep is your body's way of maintaining important cognitive skills such as speech, memory and your thought process. While asleep you move through a series of sleep phases. Each cycle consists of light sleep, deep sleep and a dream state known as REM sleep (Rapid Eye Movement). The next chapter will offer you support about how to help improve your sleep patterns.

The Bare Essentials To Help Improve Sleep

Lack of sleep may contribute towards a range of other physical or emotional issues, such as weight gain, adrenal fatigue, reduced focus, concentration and poor digestive health. There is a concept called sleep hygiene, which helps you to create an environment that is more conducive to improved sleep; I have listed some of the points below:

- Create the right temperature in your bedroom, not too warm, not too cold.
- Turn the light down low, this may help you feel more comfortable in your environment.

- Remove all electronics from your bedroom, computer, TV, mobile phone and any other electronic device; this will ensure that you remove any unwanted distractions.
- Relax in a nice hot bath and add lavender essential oil.
- Stay away from alcohol before bed, instead drink a shot glass of water for hydration.
- Meditate, be thankful and breathe in and out deeply and consistently for 5 minutes.

These are essential oils that I use for myself and my family if any of us are struggling with sleep:

- Lavender - calms relaxes and is a natural light sedative
- Roman chamomile - balances hormones; calms as a relaxant
- Vetiver - a natural sedative; very grounding and promotes tranquillity
- Cedarwood - Helps to release melatonin, which is the hormone that induces sleep

You can use essential oils in your diffuser, add two to three drops of your chosen oil and inhale, or spritz one to two drops onto your pillow. If it is for your child, mix one drop with a carrier oil for sensitive skin, and either rub underneath the soles of the feet, or gently massage on the back and forehead which will help aid relaxation.

When you inhale essential oils both topically and aromatically, this gives direct access through the brain by smell, which in turn helps relax tense muscles as well as reduce the activities of a very active mind.

Lack of sleep may also enhance the aging process, as the body is unable to rest in full. Think about what is best for you to improve your sleep pattern, and stay younger for longer.

Chapter 7

The Essentials Of Hormones And Mood Management

When stressful situations occur at home or in the workplace, many women constantly blame it on their hormones.

From the average age of 14 all the way through to your mid-sixties, you are at the beck and call of your hormones; they actually control your life.

What is a hormone?

- A circulating chemical that makes teenagers experience mood swings
- A protein-based compound that allows women to have babies
- An enzyme that raises your blood pressure when your moody teenager comes home an hour later then you had agreed

We can love them, dislike them, or feel like they are out of control, but we all know that we cannot live without our hormones. So why do we as women give our hormones such a hard time? Many hormones actually do a lot of good in our bodies; in fact they do far better than most of us probably realise. Constantly, I hear about oestrogen and progesterone. I admit that, for many years as I was growing up, I honestly thought these were the only two hormones that were created by women; how wrong I was. I started to carry out more research about female hormone imbalances when I was pregnant with my first child. I was concerned that I was suffering from mild depression. For the first few months I was very active; I continued going to the gym three times a week, and I had high levels of energy, but from month four onwards my energy levels plummeted. I felt lethargic, I struggled to feel any sense of joy, and I started to get concerned. I remember wondering if I was the only person going through this experience.

I'm sure I wasn't, but at that time in my life, I had no one else I could really share this information with. That is when I started to research hormone imbalance, and what it can do to a female on an emotional and physical level. Read on to the next chapter and find out how many hormones reside in our bodies; it is definitely more than two.

Our Hormones: The Daily Guided Tour

As you start your day, and continue organising your daily business, around 200 hormones and hormone-like substances move silently through your body. They act as chemical messengers, secreted by your major endocrine glands and other organs. Hormones affect every cell in your body, from the very basics of deciding whether you are hot or cold, feeling hungry or full, calm or stressed out, alert or tired, badly behaved or well behaved.

Whether you're asleep or awake, hormones are the building blocks to building your bones, regulating your menstrual cycle, and many other essential functions of your body. Keeping your hormones in balance is therefore a vital part of your day-to-day good health regime. As you will see below many of our major glands and hormones are inextricably linked:

- Hypothalamus -Is a small but important part of the brain. It is your control centre of the brain with a variety of functions. It plays an important role in the nervous system as well as in the endocrine system. It is linked to another small and vital gland called the pituitary gland that helps to regulate water balance, body temperature and your emotions.
- Penial - also known as the third eye and still referred to in the same way today, produces melatonin which helps maintain your sleep patterns.
- Pituitary - key endocrine glands releases at least nine major hormones, including hormones that stimulate the thyroid, adrenal glands and ovaries.
- Adrenal - if you are feeling stressed, this gland releases specialised hormones that help you whilst you are in fight or flight mode. You may have heard the term amygdala; this is part of the brain that is the size of an almond, which triggers your fight or flight or danger mode and that communicates with your adrenal glands.
- Pancreas - T cells, produce both insulin and glucagon, both hormones work together to support and regulate your blood sugar levels.
- Ovaries- there are three key hormones that are released - oestrogen, progesterone and testosterone, these hormones provide women with generous hips, your waistline, breasts, sex drive and are also responsible for causing in some women pre-menstrual tension (PMT).

When I first started researching my own hormones, I was intrigued at how each hormone has such a specific job to do in the body. As identified previously, whilst I was aware of some specific hormones, I had no clear idea about their individual responsibilities. I hope that this has helped you become a little clearer on how hormones function and play a key role within your body.

Do Hormones Affect Your Memory During Pregnancy?

During my first pregnancy, I suffered immensely with memory loss. Initially, I didn't realise that this was the case; I thought everyone around me was exaggerating my symptoms. Prior to being pregnant I never had a problem with my memory, but now I was in a senior position in my career, and memory loss hindered my role at work and at home. I discussed this with other pregnant women, I learned that this was a very common problem and I was no different than anybody else. At the time I imagined I would suffer memory loss for nine months and once I'd had my baby, my memory would revert to normal.

After the birth of my daughter, I knew that my memory was not as sharp as it used to be, and this really frustrated me. It became well known in our family that if Mum said a date or a time, it was best to always double check it as she probably got it mixed up. I would love to argue with these statements; however, there were many times when I had given incorrect information, because I had misinterpreted the time or the date. I remember taking my daughter to her best friend's party, the day after it had happened, imagine that! She was not a happy girl.

I used to question why I couldn't recall information in the same way that I could before pregnancy. Science has confirmed that pregnancy causes memory loss, and you are more forgetful at this stage of your life.

"There is 15 to 40 times more progesterone and oestrogen moving around your brain during pregnancy," Louann Brizendine, MD, director of the Women's Mood and Hormone

Clinic at the University of California, San Francisco, says. " These hormones affect all kinds of neurons in the brain. By the time the woman delivers, there are huge surges of oxytocin that cause the uterus to contract and the body to produce milk — and they also affect the brain circuits."

My biggest question after my daughter was born was if my memory would be restored. My experience was that it was not restored to the same degree. I continued to struggle remembering names, directions, dates and times. Things that I used to be able to retain in my head, I had to write down. I know this doesn't happen to all women; we are all different and this is just my experience. I believe this was a result of my imbalance of hormones, and my diet before pregnancy; my dietary intake of vegetables was inconsistent, and I was constantly eating whilst mobile. I went on maternity leave two weeks before I had my child, so my cortisol levels were extremely high. Hindsight is a wonderful word; looking back could I have done things differently? Yes; and I learned with my second child that managing my stress levels was extremely important, not only to help my child, but also for the long-term protection of my own brain and memory functionality.

If you are a mum to be, or a new mum, it will help you significantly if you invest in a good healthy diet, rich in leafy green vegetables, omega-3 and 6 essential fatty acids or flaxseeds, fruit and a constant supply of purified water. This will be a great help for both you and baby.

Why Do Your Moods Keep Changing?

This is the million-dollar question. Recalling my own experience, one minute I would feel extremely happy, and the next minute I would feel gloomy. I couldn't explain to myself why I was feeling this way; it didn't make sense to me. I would ask myself if there was something wrong with me. Then I would just put it down to my hormones. I want to share with you an overview of how your hormones work throughout a 24-hour period.

We have wake-up hormones, between 4 am and 6 am, when our body is getting ready to wake up for the day ahead. Our adrenal glands start moving into action, and start to increase the level of cortisol that is being released. Cortisol is known as the stress hormone; why would we be releasing stress at that time of the morning? Cortisol is released in small amounts throughout the day and it has its natural peaks and troughs during the day. The cortisol release before you wake up is just giving your body a gentle nudge, which slightly increases your metabolism; your body temperature rises just by a small amount so when you wake up you're alert and ready to go.

You may not have had time to have breakfast, so your blood sugar levels may have dropped, and your pancreas is now releasing glycogen, a hormone that breaks down glucose stored in your liver and muscles. Once you've had something nutritious to eat you feel much more in balance.

You continue to work up until lunchtime, and then decide to go for a quick workout at the gym. Even though it was for only 30 minutes, it was an intense workout and you feel so much better for it afterwards. Your body releases oxytocin and serotonin, which are the happy hormones, the feeling of being on top of the world hormones.

After working through the afternoon you're looking forward to getting home. The thyroid gland produces energy, and it's been very stable all day. However, you start to feel cold, and then you feel yourself warm up. This is the thyroid gland releasing more of its metabolic hormone, which is able to generate internal body warmth.

When I want to balance my blood sugar levels I use a metabolic blend of essential oils which includes grapefruit, lemon, peppermint, ginger and cinnamon. All I do is put two to three drops in water and take internally. This metabolic blend not only helps to balance my blood sugar levels, it also works as an appetite suppressant, and helps me refrain from eating items that are not of any nutritional value. Many of my clients also find this blend extremely effective, and it tastes good in water. If you prefer a healthy smoothie you can add it to that instead; whatever works best for you.

Clary Calm is an effective blend of pure essential oils that supports the reduction of hot flushes, particularly at night, as well as helping to manage emotional health.

Recognising Your Stress Level

Stress and anxiety are common experiences for most people today. When I'm feeling stressed, I'm aware that cortisol is circulating throughout my body. I'm conscious of how harmful it can be if my body is releasing significant amounts of cortisol throughout the day, which means I've entered into what's known as fight or flight mode.

These are the main changes that you may experience during this state.

- Rapid Heart Beat and Breathing: The body increases its heartbeat and you will sweat more; this provides the energy and oxygen to the body that will be used if you were in any danger.

- Pale or Flushed Skin: As the stress response starts to kick in, blood flow to certain areas of the body is reduced and the flow to the muscles, brain, legs, and arms are increased. You might become pale or ashen as a result, or your face may alternate between pale and flushed as blood rushes to your head and brain. The body's blood clotting ability also increases as this helps to prevent too much blood loss in case of an injury.
- Dilated Pupils: The body also prepares itself to be more aware of its surroundings during times of danger. When your pupils are dilated, this in turn, allows more light into the eyes, so that you have improved eyesight in case you need to see exactly what is surrounding you.
- Trembling: When you are facing a stressful or dangerous situation, your muscles become tense and ready for action. So, you start to tremble or even shake.

If your body is constantly in acute stress mode, you may suffer from any of the descriptions below, when you recognise that you are in this state, be ready to make necessary changes in order to reduce your stress levels:

- Low energy.
- Upset stomach, including diarrhoea, constipation, and nausea.
- Aches, pains, and tense muscles
- Chest pain and rapid heartbeat
- Insomnia
- Frequent colds and infections and /or headaches.
- Loss of sexual desire

The way that I manage my stress may be completely different to the way that you manage yours. It doesn't matter; we are all different. However, it's important that you recognise how harmful acute stress can be to your body, both mentally and physically.

For the next point we will explore various ways in which you may be able to reduce your stress levels.

How To Reduce And Manage Your Stress Levels

I want to outline some of the ways that have helped me and my clients through significantly stressful events in our lives.

- Sleep - getting the right amount of sleep is extremely important; when you are fully rested your body naturally replenishes itself. Getting your full six to nine hours of sleep each night is essential; in fact it's imperative that we continually seek to achieve this.
- Exercise - it may seem counterproductive as exercise can be stressful; however, it can help to relieve mental stress. It also releases hormones such as endorphins, which are chemicals that improve your mood and double up as a natural painkiller.

Following are some supplements that may help to reduce stress and anxiety.

- Ashwagandha - A herb used in Ayurvedic medicine which helps relieve anxiety
- Green tea- This has many positive attributes. Polyphenols are a part of the plant family that are very high in antioxidants, and therefore may help to reduce stress and anxiety by increasing serotonin levels.
- Valerian-valerian root is a natural sedative which may help to reduce anxiety levels.

There are many essential oils that may help reduce your feelings of stress and anxiety. Essential oils, when diffused aromatically, are extremely beneficial for affecting your mood. Here are some of the most effective essential oils that I have also shared with my clients for supporting stress reduction.

- Lavender
- Serenity (essential oil blend)
- Roman chamomile
- Vetiver
- Frankincense
- Neroli
- Sandalwood

You can use any one of these essential oils topically, but always use a carrier oil if you have a skin sensitivity. Pour 1 to 2 drops into the palm of your hand, rub your hands together and inhale. This is another great way to enhance your sense of smell, which may help you to reduce feelings of stress and anxiety.

Managing Fibroids, The Natural Way

I've met so many women who are suffering from fibroids, non-benign (non-cancerous) growths that generally form in the womb area. The growths are made up of muscle and fibrous tissue and can be the size of a pea or the size of a melon. The cause of fibroids is still relatively unknown; however, they cause so many women excruciating pain; whilst menstruating many women cannot leave the house for up to 3 days due to severe blood loss. Many are anaemic, and some women find it extremely challenging to become pregnant. Afro-Caribbean women are three times more likely to suffer from fibroids. The pain and loss of blood during the menstrual cycle becomes unbearable. Research has shown that fibroids are controlled by your hormones, both oestrogen and progesterone. It's imperative that you are aware of how to balance your hormones naturally, as this will help to ensure that you are able to manage your fibroids more effectively, whilst minimising the risk of toxins being held in the body.

When I am teaching classes about natural health to women who suffer from fibroids these are the key areas I discuss:

- Foods that help relieve the fibroids: The most informed choice is to consume organic foods. I'm aware that they are more expensive, but organic food is also pesticide and herbicide free.
- Green leafy vegetables -these vegetables are high in vitamin K which helps the blood to clot, and in turn will help manage your menstrual cycle.
- Flax seeds can help balance oestrogen levels in your body and may help to shrink the fibroids. Sprinkle flax seed on your cereal, add to your smoothie, or just eat 1 to 2 tablespoons each day.
- Natural supplements, tested for their purity and are the highest quality of ingredients which will contair Omega 3 and 6 fish oils, flaxseed oil, milk thistle and vitamin D

Certified pure essential oils:

- Frankincense - highly effective for optimum cellular health - take 2 drops twice a day in a veggie capsule with water.
- Sandalwood - highly effective for tumour reduction, spasms and cramps – diffuse in the air, and apply topically onto your reflex points use a carrier oil for skin sensitivities.
- Helichrysum - very effective for reducing heavy bleeding. This is a natural vasoconstrictor that helps the blood to coagulate. Take one to two drops in a capsule to promote healthy liver and pancreas functions; apply topically at the

back of your neck or area of concern to relieve pain and heavy bleeding.

- Lemon - highly effective for cleansing your kidneys and gallstones, this essential oil will help detox your body, take 2 to 3 drops in a veggie capsule with water internally, apply topically behind the ears to cleanse any toxins stored in your body.

Many of my clients have used dōTERRA essential oils, as well as changed their diet, re-evaluated and improved a healthy sleep pattern and embraced a basic exercise regime. Today they are happy with the improvements they have made with natural plant medicine.

Managing Hair Loss Naturally

There are numerous reasons why women suffer from hair loss. For example, weight loss, low iron levels, poor diet and stress, along with thyroid and hormone imbalances, can all cause hair to fall out. Like the rest of our body, a healthy diet and a well-functioning endocrine system is required so that your hair can flourish. There is a condition known as telogen effluvium, which occurs when the body is in shock, and causes temporary hair loss. However, generally it's restored but may take between 6 to 9 months. Polycystic ovaries, or PCOS in short, is caused by an imbalance of male and female sex hormones, and hair thinning is one of the symptoms. At my workshops I meet many women who suffer with hair loss; this condition can be both embarrassing and over time may impact your own self-esteem. Vigorous styling, and hair treatments over the years can cause your hair to fall out; for example, constant braiding, hair weaves or cornrows. Chemical relaxers or any kind of constant high heat, caused from curling tongs or hair straighteners, will also damage your hair. In fact, they can actually damage the hair roots, and sadly your hair may not grow back. Harsh hair treatments over the years may cause traction alopecia, which is triggered by chronic pulling of the hair follicle which is a result of tight braiding and cornrow hairstyles.

In order to help get the most out of your hair and maintain the lifespan of your hair follicles, always use sulphate free cleansers to help maintain the natural oils in your scalp and your hair. Look for hair products that are derived from plant-based surfactants, also known as natural saponin (foaming agents.) These are gentler on your hair and scalp, as they do not strip out the natural oils. Some examples of natural surfactants are castile soap, yucca extract, and coconut oil. Outlined below is a homemade blend that I use to help keep my hair healthy. To avoid sensitivities always mix in a glass jar, with 50% organic carrier oil, coconut oil or shea butter.

- **Frankincense 20 drops** – highly effective at promoting a healthy scalp, and moisturising existing hair follicles to support the prevention of further hair loss
- **Geranium 15 drops** -is best known for strengthening the hair follicles and individual strands
- **Melaleuca 15 drops** - commonly known as tea tree oil, helps to encourage hair growth by cleansing damaged or clogged hair follicles, and reducing dandruff
- **Rosemary 5 drops** - strengthens circulation and stimulates the hair follicles (avoid use whilst pregnant)
- **Bergamot oil 10 drops** - has anti-microbial properties that help keep scalp infections away, very calming on the scalp, mind and nervous system.
- **Carrier Oils** - use 2 tbsp of either - Almond Oil, Jojoba, Coconut, Olive Oil (or another)

Blend together and use as part of your hair conditioning regime, or blend with shea butter, and use small amounts as a daily hair food, which will continue to add moisture to your hair.

Managing Menopause Naturally

Women in general don't just suddenly hit upon menopause; when we are perimenopausal this means we are building up to the full change of menopause. Unless you are prescribed certain medications, it is far from an immediate change, but will happen over time. It is different for every woman. Some women will go through years of hormonal imbalance, which will peak and then plummet. You may not experience a period in 3 to 4 months and suddenly you bleed for 2 or 3 days, and you may be confused by your bodily experience. The perimenopause period may last anywhere between 2 to 8 years, and typically begins in your 40's. I have met some women who began in their 30's, and some who started in their 50's. The variation is vast, and individual to each female. Hormonal imbalance starts off subtle; however, fluctuations of oestrogen may become extreme, and then fall to very low levels. When you have not experienced a period for a minimum of one year, you have started menopause. For many women this may consist of hot flushes, low sex drive, brain fog, constant tiredness, and increased joint and muscle pain. This is nature's time for transition, and you may find benefits from changing your diet. Think about Including good quality vitamins and minerals, which will help keep your bones strong. This is vital, due to oestrogen reduction in the body which may result in brittle bones, and many women are at a higher risk of osteoporosis. Here are some of the natural resources that may help with menopause:

- Clary Calm - calming blend of pure essential oils - Provides a soothing and calming effect during menopause, its calming aroma helps soothe and balance heightened emotions. Helps balance mood throughout the month and supports hot flushes. A mix of clary sage, bergamot, lavender, Roman chamomile, and ylang ylang essential oils.

- Black Cohosh – Black cohosh, also known as black snakeroot or bugbane, is a medicinal root. It is used to treat women's hormone-related symptoms, including premenstrual syndrome (PMS), menstrual cramps, and menopausal symptoms.
- Soy Isoflavones (Non-GMO) – Soy is high in isoflavones. Isoflavones are a type of phytoestrogen. Phytoestrogens are chemicals found in plants that work like oestrogens. These ingredients are deemed safe as a dietary supplement, however, carry out your own phytoestrogen research as I'm aware that soy is still a controversial subject.
- Organic Liquorice Root – This contains Glycyrrhizin, which helps to increase oestrogen levels in women when they are too low, this comes in the root, herb or a powder format.

These are foods you can eat that will help you manage your menopause symptoms: artichokes, asparagus, avocado, tomatoes, spinach, broccoli, Brussels sprouts, cucumber, olives and cabbage, probiotic yogurts and kefir, organic eggs, herring, wild salmon and sardines, almonds, coconut, pine nuts, walnuts, hazelnuts and flax seed. Juicing is also very beneficial for cleansing your system, and organic bone broth can be effective for guarding against osteoporosis.

Chapter 8

Men's Health And Chronic Pain

For many men chronic inflammation is known as a silent killer. Chronic inflammation has the ability to flood your body without you realising what's happening. Your immune system cannot keep up with the constant demands, and as you mature and get older your cells do not regenerate in the same way they did in your younger years. This in turn places far more stress on your immune system, and in many cases can be the route of much more serious diseases such as heart disease, Alzheimer's disease, cancer, depression and stroke.

There are different forms of inflammation, and acute inflammation is not the same as chronic inflammation. Acute information may occur if you have been cycling, working out at the gym, hiking, or even decorating. In my experience inflammation of the tendons in your legs is also common. In this instance you could apply topically to the area of discomfort Roman chamomile, peppermint or camphor essential oil (use a carrier oil in case of any skin sensitivity). Use a cold or warm compress, depending on your bodily requirements. This will help reduce the inflammation and soothe away any lactide acid residue, some well-earned rest.

My husband was a basketball player and suffered a back injury during his younger years. At that time of his life, as with many young men, he thought nothing of the injury and believed that over time it would heal itself. Fast forward 30 years and my husband still suffers from back pain, and he knows that this is due to the accident/ injury that occurred when he was playing basketball. We have always researched holistic, complementary remedies.

The approach taken was to engage with a chiropractor regularly, invest in deep tissue massage, continue to exercise and eat a healthier diet which for him meant cutting down on sugary foods, as this exacerbated the inflammation. Whilst he still suffers from an occasional backache or lower back pain, the symptoms have significantly reduced. Primarily this is due to conscious changes in his diet, along with natural supplements and a blend of therapeutic grade anti-inflammatory essential oils called Deep Blue Rub.

You may have already started to make changes to your lifestyle, which should include your diet and quality natural supplements to enhance your overall wellness. Introduce an exercise regime; this doesn't have to be overly intense. In order to increase your level of flexibility, it is critical to include stretching movements. Keep your water intake constant to avoid dehydration, and become more aware of which activities increase your stress levels. Learn to recognise those triggers; stop ignoring them as this will only increase the level of inflammation over a longer period of time. This is about being more aware and in tune with your body, so that you take control and concentrate on becoming the healer of your own body system.

Looking After Your Prostate

From the age of 25 your prostate begins to grow. This is not unusual, and this natural growth is called benign prostatic hyperplasia (BPH),and for many men it goes somewhat unnoticed early on. However, when you reach the age of 40+, for many men the recognition of potential prostate issues becomes more prominent. BPH is a benign condition that does not lead to prostate cancer, although the two problems can coexist. But 50% of men with BPH may never develop any symptoms. This is good news as many men are led to believe that they will develop some form of prostate concern around the age of 40. However, others may find that BPH can make their life unbearable. Some of the symptoms are listed below:

- A weak urine stream
- A sense of incomplete emptying
- The urge to frequently urinate particularly at night time

You will be pleased to know that there are some tips for relieving these symptoms, starting with your diet. It has been scientifically proven that cruciferous vegetables are extremely effective for natural prostate reduction:

- Broccoli
- Cauliflower
- Brussels sprouts
- Cabbage
- Kale
- Chilli Peppers

I know this may sound simple, but when you go to the bathroom ensure that you empty your bladder as much as possible, as this will help enhance your feeling of release and reduce the number of times you need to frequent the bathroom. If stress is a constant factor for you, then you may benefit from listening to soothing music, or practicing meditation and focusing on your breathing techniques. It helps reduce feelings of stress, and it may also help reduce the number of times you feel you need to urinate.

Ensure that you avoid drinking too much fluid in the evening; practice a clear cut-off point in your mind so that you know when your last intake of fluid will be, particularly caffeinated and alcoholic drinks. Both can affect the muscle tone of your bladder and both stimulate your kidneys to produce urine, in turn leads to you getting up in the night and heading for the bathroom.

The Bare Essentials – Supporting your Prostate

If you are open to natural essential oil remedies, you may want to find out more about the prostate relief blend which is listed below. Again, please note that I am only discussing dōTERRA essential oils, as these are the essential oils that my family and I use.

- Apply two to three drops of Balance, the grounding blend, to the bottoms of your feet morning and evening before you go to sleep.
- Consume one drop of Frankincense, two to three times daily. This helps to promote brain and prostrate health.
- Apply two to three drops of cellular complex blend topically on your feet (focusing on the heel area) lower abdomen, and inner thigh. This blend helps to support cellular repair, and prostrate relief.
- Apply two drops of juniper berry essential oil onto your abdomen are. Use a carrier oil if you have a skin sensitivity; apply this in the morning and at night time. This supports urinary and prostrate health as well as incorporating wound healing properties.
- Raw unfiltered, organic apple cider vinegar is very effective, as it has astringent properties that help reduce swollen prostate glands. This may taste a little on the bitter side; however, you only require a few drops in a small glass. This

is effective for many types of inflammation, and the most effective times to take it are in the morning and before bedtime. Men tend to be more independent by nature; you may be less likely to make an appointment to see your doctor. Therefore, by empowering yourself with the knowledge of natural remedies, you can practice this at any time and help yourself manage your own health risk whilst maintaining a better body balance overall. Ensure that you always seek medical help when it is necessary.

Recently I was introduced to a man that I will call James, who very kindly shared with me that he had been diagnosed with early stages of prostate cancer three months ago. James received regular check ups; in fact, he was the one that chased his GP, James was not contacted for his annual check-up for over a year, after his delayed appointment James was informed that he had the onset of prostate cancer. James had an operation, which was a success, then he went through the recovery process, which entailed having a colostomy bag fitted, which held his urine as those muscles where no longer effective. He had to practice pelvic floor exercises with a large group of other men in the hospital to improve his muscle management for erectile dysfunction. James also had to wear a male nappy, due to incontinence, and this was at least 12 weeks after the operation, by which time he had returned to work.

The reason why James shared his story with me was to spread the message and ensure that all men request regular prostate checks. He told me that he had to get over the embarrassment of feeling like a child again, and that it was more important to share the facts of prostrate with other men so that they can avoid experiencing a similar process. James is currently happy and healthy, as he still has the gift of life.

Disclaimer: None of the above information is suggested to replace any medical advice that you may have received from your doctor.

What Is Happening In My Gut?

The key food culprit is sugar. I can hear you saying, oh no, not sugar again, I love sugar! But sugar is hidden in so many products; how do you know? It may seem tedious, but it's worth reading the labels before you make your purchase, so that you are aware of what you're putting in your body. Sugar is like a sweet poison; it corrodes your gut. When you are influenced by a high sugar and high fat diet your gut bacteria grows negatively, and this allows harmful species to overgrow in your gut. Once you regularly feed the wrong bacteria, it's a bit like if you don't keep your garden under control; the weeds start to grow rapidly. After a week or two, look outside and the weeds have totally overgrown in your garden and strangled the grass. You could use a similar analogy for what happens in the gut, when bad bacteria are able to grow at a faster rate than the good bacteria.

Harmful bacteria may also cause you to absorb more calories. If you feel that you have a balance of healthy gut bacteria, just be mindful when you are consuming antibiotics as they may reduce your level of good bacteria. It is not all doom and gloom, however. Fermented yoghurt and other fermented foods are a great source of natural probiotics, and these are readily available in many natural health stores and supermarkets.

Probiotics are a beneficial bacterium which you need, and prebiotics are a source of food for these bacteria. To explain this in a little more detail, probiotics are live bacteria found in certain foods or supplements which can provide numerous health benefits, particularly for the gut. Good gut bacteria in your digestive tract will help to protect you from many kinds of harmful bacteria and fungi.

Many of my clients use a pre and probiotic called PB Assist. You consume one capsule before a meal. This is a slow-release prebiotic, and after a period of time the probiotic is released into your digestive system.

Think about including a digestive enzyme in your daily diet, as the digestive enzyme will help break down the food in your gut. This is extremely important as sometimes we forget that our stomach doesn't have teeth. Most people do not chew their food 25 times or more; therefore, that piece of meat that has been consumed sits dormant in the gut; and eventually will turn rancid, and may cause further problems.

Make a conscious decision to become more aware of your gut health and what you're eating; cut back where possible on unhealthy foods and drinks, including caffeine and alcohol that over time may exacerbate your gut concerns.

There are a range of dōTERRA essential oils that may help support your gut health. These are ginger, peppermint, cardamom, fennel, and a blend known as Zengest that includes all the gut support oils. These can be used topically and applied over the stomach area or across the throat, depending on your symptoms (always use a carrier oil for any skin sensitivity). You can put two drops in an empty veggie cap and ingest with a small glass of water, and the oils will work synergistically in your body and will target and reach every cell. Now is the time to become more aware of what you are putting into your body as you truly are what you eat.

Why Am I Losing My Hair?

Hair loss and baldness is a common condition that develops in most men at some stage of their life. Typically, the hair begins to thin or recede at the sides and on top of the head. Generally, a bald patch starts to develop in the middle of the scalp, and may increase in size and eventually join with the receding sections on each side, leaving a patch at the front. There is no known cause for hair loss or baldness; however, studies show that there are some common trends.

Hair is made in hair follicles that lie under the skin surface. A hair will usually grow from each follicle for about 3 to 5 years; once the cycle is complete, the old hair is shed, and a new hair will start to grow. The cycle of hair growth and shedding continues throughout life. The following factors tend to affect men as they become bald. The hair follicles gradually become smaller as the follicles shrink, and each new hair becomes thinner than the previous strand. Prior to falling out, each new hair grows for less time than the normal 3 years. Hair loss and baldness have a range of causes, all of which may differ with each individual.

For some men it could be attributed to their hormones; the level of the male hormone testosterone is normal in men with baldness. However, cells in the scalp convert testosterone into another hormone called Dihydrotestosterone or DHT. Hair loss is also a hereditary condition and is commonly called male pattern baldness, which also affects the age at which you begin to lose hair, and the rate at which you lose your hair.

As we age, hair loss can become a natural process. Hair can begin to shrink in both length and diameter, which causes it to shed, and the actual follicular units to decrease in number. Stress can also cause hair loss; however, this hair loss is not permanent. There are different types of hair loss that are related to stress; the most common is known as telogen effluvium. The hair stops growing during telogen effluvium and lies dormant, it starts falling out 2 to 3 months later, and within 6 to 9 months it begins to grow back.

Alopecia areata is a disease that causes hair to fall out in small patches. It develops when the immune system attacks the hair follicles, resulting in hair loss. Sudden hair loss may occur on the scalp and other parts of the body, including eyebrows and eyelashes.

Androgenic alopecia is another cause of hair loss, occurring when white blood cells attach to hair follicles. It leads to fast hair loss and often occurs in patches. Within weeks the whole scalp can lose hair. In many cases the hair grows back, but sometimes further treatment is required.

If you are unsure about the cause of your hair loss, you may wish to visit a trichologist or a dermatologist, for further support.

The Bare Essentials – Maintaining Your Hair

As you have discovered, there are many different reasons that cause hair loss. If you are looking at trying something new, you may want to introduce essential oils into your routine. Always blend with a good organic carrier oil such as coconut oil, olive oil, Moroccan argan oil or jojoba oil. It's also important to do your own research and look for sulphate-free and paraben-free hair products, as these chemicals can be harmful to your hair. Below are some essential oils that will help support your hair maintenance regime.

- **Melaleuca** - commonly known as tea tree oil, will help to encourage hair growth by cleansing damaged or clogged hair follicles. Dandruff can also play a factor in clogged hair follicles, so the oil will help to clean out hair roots and further prevent any itching or inflammation that may cause premature hair loss.
- **Lavender** - when massaged into the scalp, it helps improve blood circulation, and promotes hair growth. Furthermore, it is a powerful moisturiser, antimicrobial and antiseptic. It moisturises the scalp and helps to balance sebum production.
- **Peppermint** - increases blood flow, helps rejuvenate hair follicles which may stimulate hair growth. Its cleansing properties unclogs pores and allows for the normal flow of skin cells, which makes it perfect for those with a dry scalp.
- **Cedarwood** - An ideal essential oil for hair, as it balances the oil producing glands of the scalp. This warming oil significantly improves blood circulation and has a calming effect on the scalp. Furthermore, it's antibacterial and antiseptic which helps manage fungal problems and the build-up of dandruff.
- **Vetiver** – aids in the reduction of hair loss resulting from excessive heat in the body. Stress can cause the body to become overheated, as well as compromising your immune system. The soothing and calming effects of this earthy, root plant, helps to cool the body and calm the mind, which can result in reduced levels of stress

Why not try the DIY Hair Maintenance Blend below?

- 6 drops of Lavender essential oil
- 1 drop of Peppermint essential oil
- 3 drops of Cedarwood essential oil
- 1 drop of Vetiver essential oil
- 2 tbsp warm, coconut carrier oil (or your choice of carrier oil)

- Massage the blend into the scalp, use a towel or cap to cover your head
- Rinse out conditioner after 2 hours
- Try this once a week; it should help add moisture to your hair, reduce any itchiness caused by dandruff or a dry scalp, and help further stimulate your hair follicles.

Managing Stress And Anxiety

Stress must be taken seriously, because it affects so many of us. My experience with male clients, as identified previously, is that men tend to internalize stress and anxiety and what is really bothering them, much more than women. It may be due to how you were raised, or the messages you heard. For instance:

- be the man
- man up
- stop crying, that's for girl's

However, as you mature and accept more and more of life stressors, there has to be a release. Otherwise it may manifest itself into a health condition, and you really want to avoid that outcome.

I know this may be easy for me to say, and you've probably heard it many times before; stress and anxiety are two of the most dangerous health conditions as many go undetected and unrecognised by you. Stress has become such a common word, which is spoken about many times during the day, and it is a fact that continues to affect men's health. Anxiety and the emotional strain of day-to-day living has been linked to heart disease, high blood pressure, chronic migraines, headaches, back pain, diabetes, cancer, and a weakened immune system. This also includes insomnia and fatigue, and on rare occasions, mild depression which may subsequently lead to unhealthy habits such as drinking, smoking, overindulging in food, or even drug abuse.

That is not to say that stress and anxiety doesn't exist for other people; in many cases it does. How you manage and deal with it on an ongoing basis is the key to staying healthy and in balance with your body. There are many ways to do this, and it's not a one size fits all; you will have your preference of how you like to reduce feelings of stress and anxiety. In case you feel like trying something new, I have a few suggestions that I have discussed with previous clients who have found my ideas of some help.

- Exercise regularly; this may help you to burn off pent up energy and tension, and it will also improve your overall health.
- Ensure you eat and sleep well; good nutrition is always important. Six to nine hours of sleep each night can help your body recover from past stress and be better prepared to deal with anything that the day has to offer.
- Avoid caffeine and alcohol; caffeine may promote feelings of stress and it will be far more challenging for you to relax and sleep.
- Sit in silence for a minimum of 5 to 10 minutes. If this is new to you, then find a quiet space that is comfortable without any disturbances.
- Depending on your preference you may like to practice a form of Martial arts or Tai Chi or you may just want to sit quietly and continue to breathe deeply; select whatever you feel works for you.

The key is to start and include whatever you choose into your daily routine.

A great way to induce clarity and calmness, in a meditative state is to start inhaling essential oils. Frankincense is incredibly effective for meditation and supports clarity and stress reduction. Petitgrain, which is known for many benefits including reducing stress and anxiety, is a natural sedative and will aid restful sleep. This is not about making major changes; it's more about implementing incremental adjustments that you will sustain to stay healthier.

Chapter 9

Being Grateful For Your Blessings

There are days when I find myself focusing on what is going wrong with my day, and I start to question myself: Why is this happening to me today? What have I done to deserve this? As soon as these thoughts manifest in my mind, I know that if I don't want this thought process to continue, then I need to take a minute or two to refocus my thoughts and my energy levels. Change what I'm thinking to reflect on the positive areas that I've experienced that day, and there is always at least one that I can find.

The fact that I can get up in the morning, breathe deeply and meditate, and inhale my wonderful therapeutic grade essential oils is an absolute blessing.

I can choose to feel happiness and appreciation when the rain starts to fall, instead of thinking I'm going to get wet when I leave the house. I replace that thought with how amazing it is that the grass looks greener, the flowers are being nourished, nature is having a shower, and replenishing all that we need to breathe in the air that surrounds us. Nature continues to offer us the ability to live our abundant lives.

How often do you take a few minutes of your day to sit down and think about the happiness that has touched your life? It is so easy to start your day with feelings of frustration, and continue your day thinking about the negative actions of other people, and how they have had a negative impact on your day. As I have mentioned previously, you are an energetic being; when your energy is low, your vibration is low, and what that means is that you will continue to attract negative or unpleasant experiences. Some of the teachings in my book explain what you could do in order to elevate your thought process, and focus your energy on the joys of your day. You may be thinking I haven't experienced any joy today; think again, there will be something that you will find, even if it was for a brief moment that made you smile internally or externally.

I'm aware that some days it can be extremely challenging to feel any level of optimism, but being grateful reminds you that there are people supporting you. It may not be a family member; it maybe somebody outside of your family, a work colleague or a therapist. It could even be a stranger that you shared a few words with during the day, and those few words have really helped you. This is the encouragement that you require; these soul angels have helped you through your tough times. Remember, it's important to recognise and honour them for what they have gifted to you. Even though it may seem somewhat small to that individual, it has helped you to shine your light in a much brighter fashion.

Challenges are a part of our daily life, and as you are experiencing those challenges, you may not appreciate the learning that is there for your reflection. You are so encompassed in the situation that it's very hard to look from the outside in. Yet the challenges are often the very things that can help define, improve, alter and sometimes force necessary changes and growth in you as an individual. Don't forget to acknowledge your challenges, what you have learnt, and most importantly what you are grateful for. This demonstrates true gratitude for each of your life experiences.

Incorporate Love In All That You Do

What does the word love mean to you? How do you define love? I define love as a feeling like no other; for me it is euphoric and exhilarating, an absolute daydream state. It genuinely feels like there are one or two butterflies speed-skating in the pit of my stomach, and for me there is no better feeling. I love my husband, I love my children, my brother, my friends and my wider family, and on a professional level my clients. Within those descriptions there are variations of love, but it's still love. As I've gotten older, I also experience love for those that are not in my close circle. I guess this is more of an altruistic love for other human beings, the beautiful world of nature, and an unconditional love for God and the universe.

When you start to incorporate love in all that you do and say, you are naturally vibrating on a higher energetic frequency, which will enable you to feel more empathy for other people, as well be less hard on yourself. If something in your life has not gone to plan, it doesn't really matter. It's the constant feeling of appreciation that matters, and it's a very good place to be. Love is a powerful emotion; in fact in my opinion it's the most powerful of emotions. There is nothing that supersedes the feeling of love.

Whether it's a person, an animal or an object such as a car that evokes these feelings within you, know that it is love. There is a great book called "The Five Languages of Love" by Gary Chapman. In this book, he talks about the five languages of love and how individuals interpret that language and receive love or perceived love. I've outlined them below:

Words of Affirmation: For many people, hearing I love you or another compliment is what they find of the most value. Words mean everything within this language; this is not to forget that negative or hurtful comments will be held deeply and won't be easily forgiven.

Quality Time: This is very much about giving the other person your undivided attention, no matter how short a time that might be. Any distractions or the feeling of not being heard or listened to may be damaging for this individual, so being there in the present is extremely important.

Gifts: To some people what makes them feel most loved is to receive a gift; this is what makes them feel most appreciated. That is not selfish in any way; it is their preference.

Acts of Service: Actions speak so much louder than words. Anything service orientated is very important; dealing with broken promises or perceive laziness is not really tolerated as it gives more work to that individual, so if you're not willing to show your appreciation by doing them a favour it feels as if you do not value them as a person.

Physical Touch: There's nothing that speaks more deeply than appropriate touch, and that could be stroking your hair, holding hands, a slight touch of the leg. It's that safety feeling that makes them feel safe and loved.

Keep your vibrations high and see if you recognise your own love languages.

Abundance Is All Around You

What is the definition of abundance? It is a very large quantity of something; for example, the tropical island of Belize boasts an abundance of wildlife. To me abundance means there is no difference between love, money or power; it is the intention that you attach to each of these words. Living an abundant life is yours for the taking; you always have a choice. I recognise that there are times in your life when it may not feel this way.

I specifically remember one of my clients who had a very negative outlook on the world. This went back to his childhood, how he was raised, and how his parents saw the world, which in turn was passed down to him. He decided that he wanted to break the cycle, in order that his children could have a more positive outlook on life. We worked intensely over a period of time, and finally towards the end of our sessions, he shared this thought with me: "For the first time in my life I've started to think about what I have to be grateful for, what I've helped to create, and I'm realising that I can apply my thought process to everything I do, and it just feels better." His life started to shift in a positive direction as he recognised the power of his thoughts, and making the choice between luck and cynicism or abundance and positivity.

You may think you're living abundantly; however, your subconscious mind, which controls 90% of your thought process, demonstrates in reality you are living in lack; you have chosen to live a life of scarcity. I want you to think about that for a couple of minutes and be honest with yourself; are you just using the word abundance? Or are you truly living and breathing those words? There is a big difference, and you will recognise deeply within yourself where you really are. If you're reading this paragraph and saying to yourself I'm not sure what I feel, then give yourself the time to think again; sit down and ask the question, and answer yourself honestly.

Abundance is all around you. It may be true that you cannot necessarily see it; however, it is there. So, embrace love instead of fear; embrace spirit instead of sadness; embrace service instead of constant consumption. This may not be a natural standpoint for you and that's fine; if you really want to experience abundance and make a difference in the world, then any one of the three points that I have highlighted is an effective way to start.

One of the things that I love is when I'm speaking on stage and I've sat down on a chair, ready to do a guided meditation with my audience. It is always short, but it's also powerful. After my talk, many people approach me and thank me for sharing what they recognise as words of encouragement, love and compassion. Sometimes all we need is for somebody else around us to share their vision; share their words of enlightenment and reassurance, so that we can comfort and nourish ourselves and pass our abundant energy forward.

Recognising Your Power

There have been many times in my life when I have felt unheard, and unworthy of being listened to. During those times, I believed that I was made to feel this way by other people, and that for some reason they either disliked me or maybe felt threatened by my presence.

This was my interpretation. In fact it was nothing to do with the other people; it was my own beliefs that had me feeling this way. In those situations, I felt totally disempowered. As I continued my journey of life, I came to recognise that I was still reliving old situations going back to childhood that I thought I had resolved. The same triggers were allowing me to feel uncomfortable and ineffective, as if I were still 9 years old. I also believe that coupled with this was the physical loss of my voice. In my opinion this was due to my decision not to truly express what was on my mind in case it upset other people. This confirmed my cycle of disempowerment, which in turn left me feeling unheard, and it would subsequently start the cycle all over again.

I remember in my early days working as a therapist, one of my first clients was from Latin America, and her upbringing was heavily focused around religion; as a child she was never able to make her own decisions and was taught that to be kind and selfless was all that really mattered. She would share and give all her possessions away, and this had followed her throughout her life and now into her adult life. This way of being was no longer serving its purpose, as she continued to give all her possessions away; including money that was meant for her food and rent.

We worked together on changing those habits through her thought process, language when speaking to herself, role play and really thinking about the consequences of each action as a selfless act. I supported my client for 7 months, and she persevered and made all the necessary changes that allowed her to not only release those limiting beliefs that were no longer serving her, but also to find her voice, regain her power, and start to make beneficial informed decisions in her everyday life. Have you ever felt that you have given away your power to others? This is very common in today's world. Everything is labelled; you are either successful or unsuccessful, attractive or unattractive. There is no in-between. You are pressured by society to fit into neat little boxes that have been created to recognise what others see as your normality. Each time you place yourself into the box you close the lid on your own individuality and power. So why not try something new? When making a decision, ask yourself: Does this decision come from my inner self and truth, or is this decision coming from what society will think of me?

Express how you feel and don't blame others. This may be challenging the first few times that you think about it, but it is not impossible to do. Allow yourself to be open and vulnerable, and have the courage to express your true feelings and your needs. Get to know yourself, and what you want. Once you find your inner light, it will act like your own body compass and will always guide you in the right direction. Follow the path that your life flow takes you on; it's an incredible feeling knowing that you have the power, so own it and let those around you know that it's yours.

Finding Your Purpose

I've been to many seminars, workshops, and weekend retreats, all in the name of finding my purpose. I have talked to many other people about what they did, and changes they had made in their lives, and at that time, it seemed to me that everybody had found their purpose except me. I would get so frustrated with myself. I would constantly ask myself: What is my purpose? Why am I here? It was as if I was demanding an answer through the meditative process, even though I'm not sure exactly what I was expecting to hear. I want to share this as I recognise that many people, whether they are clients or friends that I speak to, are being hard on themselves by thinking that they should know exactly what their purpose is, and what they are here to do.

It took me many years to truly identify what I believe is my purpose, which is sharing the message of natural health and well-being with my family, my wider community, and the world. Prior to this I had worked for a range of companies, always supporting young people and adults, either to gain qualifications or to find other employment. Whilst I was blessed to be a part of those people's lives and the organisations I had worked for, I knew there was something else; I wasn't sure what that something else was, but I always felt there was something missing. For me, the time came when I had to decide about starting again, and either creating a career of love or staying with the money, which ultimately made life much easier. I made the decision that I needed to be fulfilled in my passion and my purpose, so I took a huge leap of faith and left a very good career of 20 years behind me. I had no job to go to, and I remember just how free I felt when I left my office for the last time. I retrained as a lifestyle coach and a therapist, I entered my own world of natural health, and I've never looked back. I'm not going to pretend that there haven't been times of severe doubt, anxiety and stress, wondering if I done the right thing. My soul voice, my intuition, always supported me, and I knew that I had made the right decision; I just needed to keep believing it.

In my experience there is no easy way, or simple steps, to find your purpose; you need to know what is meaningful for you. What kind of life have you lived? What experiences have you had? How can you share your story with others? Some of it may be painful, but there will be always others experiencing a similar type of pain. Your future reflects how you're living today. If you feel your life path is about leaving a legacy for your children, your family, your friends and making an impact in this world, yet you are unsure about what kind of impact you wish to make, then you need to peel back your layers, just like an onion, and find out what keeps you from knowing this. Sit with your thoughts, your feelings, your culture, your core beliefs, your value system, and within that complex arena of emotions, if there are some areas that continue keeping you in a place of uncertainty, don't be afraid to ask for help.

It can be quite a daunting task trying to work this out on your own. Seek out a therapist; they are there to help you gain clarity and unpack the questions that you need the answers to. You may need to try many different things before you'll find something that you love and you would happily do for free if you could afford it; if it feels like love, or it fills you with hope and joy, and you share that positivity every day, then without even realising it you have truly begun to live your life's purpose.

It Only Takes Two Minutes

Many times my clients have said to me, I don't have the time, and I generally respond by saying If this is important to you then you will find a way to make the time. This is not just my clients; I find that I also mirror these words, and I catch myself saying I just haven't got the time today; then I engage in my own self-talk and I ask myself these two questions:

1. Do I want to make this change in my life?
2. Am I certain that I can't find the time?

This is true for most of us. This train of thought takes less than a minute, but it can change the way you live your life for the better.

There is a great line in a book called "You Can Heal Your Life" by Louise Hay:

I am safe. All is well. Everything comes to me at the right time. I know that took only a few seconds to read, so I'm going to give you a list of 6 short, easy-to-remember daily affirmations. They may help you to become more focused and effective, and assist you in experiencing a greater satisfaction of inner peace. The best times to read these are in the morning or evening (depending on your work pattern). Doing this will help you get into a daily routine. Repeat each affirmation at least twice; do this consistently for the next seven days and then review and see how you're feeling:

1. I am enough
2. I wake up happy and productive
3. My body is healing itself everyday
4. I love and approve of myself
5. My life serves a purpose
6. I am worthy of happiness and respect

If you really want to focus your attention, along with your positive affirmations, use the following dōTERRA pure essential oils:

- Frankincense - highly effective for meditation and clarity
- Roman chamomile - supports emotional balance, helps transport you from feeling frustrated to feeling purposeful.
- Bergamot - helps to transport you from feeling inadequate to feelings of worthiness. Put two drops in the palm of your hand and inhale, then start your affirmations and you will notice how effective this process becomes in your life. You can do this every day, as it only takes 2 minutes, give yourself permission to take 2 minutes for yourself at the start of your day.

Chapter 10

Always Speak Your Authentic Truth

You Finally Found Your Voice

If you have been following my helpful tips and guidance throughout my book, and have made a conscious decision to absorb yourself in natural healing with essential oils, wild orange, bergamot, ylang ylang and peppermint are just some of the essential oils that are incredibly uplifting.

Finding your authentic voice in certain situations may still prove to be a challenge; for example, speaking out loud in a large team meeting, requesting a salary increase, or speaking to an ex-partner who did not respect you in the way that you deserved.

To help you speak your truth, try blending these essential oils together, along with a tbsp of fractionated coconut oil: frankincense, wild orange, and lavender. Mix three drops of each essential oil in with the fractionated coconut oil and rub topically all over the front of your neck and around the back of your neck, touching the top of your shoulders. This blend should help clear your throat, and allows your internal voice to confirm the confidence that you hold in your own abilities to speak your truth. Your words are spoken more easily and effortlessly. This is your time to shine, so refrain from allowing others to tell you what is best for you. This is not to say that you shouldn't accept good advice; it can be very helpful to gain an external opinion, but ultimately the final decision of what you wish to say should be yours.

I remember going through the process of learning how to say NO to people; I had become a serial people pleaser. Saying the word no to people, when they asked for my help in any way, was extremely difficult. It was a true challenge for me. The word no got stuck in my throat and for many years, even though I thought about saying no, the word yes continually rolled out of my mouth. Like anything, it takes practice. When you get used to saying no, and giving a brief explanation for your answer, eventually it becomes more manageable. I hesitate to say that I'm always comfortable, however. There are situations with family members when I still find it uncomfortable to say no. I recognise that this is a work in progress, and I will continue to question my judgement, so that I feel at ease with my choice of words.

Saying no doesn't mean that your friend, acquaintance or work colleague will think any less of you. In some cases, it has the opposite effect, and you will gain more respect for being honest. It also feels much more authentic when you do say yes, as your inner or wider circle begin to realise that you have thought long and hard about your decision, and that speaks volumes. Speak up for what you want, and don't be afraid of being persistent; this is yet another way of owning your power. If you need to think clearly about your answer, take a minute to be silent, and allow those around you to absorb it too. When you are ready with a clear and concise response to the question that you have been asked, give your authentic reply with good intention. It may feel somewhat uncomfortable, but practice makes it easier to manage the next time it happens. Now that you have found your voice, what more can you do with it to help you and those around you flourish in the future?

Remove the Rocks From Your Backpack

After working very hard for a prolonged period of time, I decided that I needed to take a short break, so I booked a weekend retreat to Devon, which is a beautiful part of the English countryside. I was asked, by the group I was with, to take a long walk that included some rough terrain, but I knew it would be very exhilarating, and also provide some time for silence and contemplation. I was also asked to carry a rucksack on my back, filled with stones and rocks. At the time I thought this was a strange request, but I had decided to go with the flow of the weekend, so I agreed.

We set off on our walk. At first, I was fine for a good distance of the walk, and my rocks and stones did not feel too heavy; but as we continued on with what had changed to more of a hike, the hills became steeper and I started to struggle. I was hot, and I was sweating. I experienced a shortness of breath, and I wanted to start taking the rocks out of my backpack. We were able to do this whenever we felt it was appropriate, but there was a competitive part of me that didn't want to start removing my rocks prior to anyone else, even though I knew that I was misinterpreting the task.

Eventually I started to take the rocks out, one by one, and of course it felt much lighter, and my back and shoulders felt much more flexible. My whole body felt lighter, and when we reached the top of the hill we sat down. As we spoke, each of us began to realise that these stones and rocks we were carrying in our backpacks represented the baggage that we carried with us every day. That was the learning that I acquired from this exercise, which was highly effective for me. When I brought this technique into my everyday life, it made a profound impact on my ability to release negative energy and restore my mindset.

As we experience our own trials and tribulations, unintentionally, many of us carry around an invisible backpack full of rocks and stones, that over the years have created an unnecessarily heavy load. When I'm working with my clients, one-on-one or in a group setting, I incorporate this exercise. We spend time unpacking the stones and the rocks, and allowing the release of that blocked energy; recognising that now is the time to let it go. You need to realise that you are not bound to your backpack, unless you choose to be.

Very few people wake up thinking, I want to carry around a backpack full of rocks today and for the next 5,10,15 or 20 years; however, as life plays itself out this is what many of us tend to do. I want you to really think about the stones and rocks that you are still carrying from your past, that are still appearing in your present. If you are strong enough and you feel fit and able, why not do this as an actual exercise? Take a rucksack, place a small amount of rocks and stones inside, and walk to your nearest park or to your nearest forest or woodland area. As you think about what you're still carrying, remove your stones and rocks one by one, and release any thoughts and emotions that no longer serve you. When you're finished, allow yourself around 20 to 30 minutes of reflection time; feel the feelings and praise yourself with positive thoughts and affirmations. Allow nature to nurture you, during this time of thought and much needed emotional release.

Refuse To Be Invisible

Many times in the past, I have allowed myself to believe that what I wanted to express was of little value to others. I have found myself in a group of people fluently conversant, and seemingly knowledgeable about a subject that I believed I knew very little about. It was as if I was looking from the outside in;

even though I was part of the conversation I had disassociated myself from the discussion. This wasn't due to the conversing group; it was my own thought process, and what I assumed other people would think about my own lack of knowledge. Subsequently the frustration that I experienced was that even though I had a worthwhile contribution to offer, I had chosen to be invisible.

Like many of life's challenges, this stems back to my childhood. Whenever I became worried or concerned I would internalise my feelings. I was a very sensitive child, but that was not the image that I portrayed to the world. I was raised in foster care with my brother, so externally I had to be tough and show the world, in my own childish way, that I was fearless. However, in reality I was just the opposite. All I wanted to do was feel safe and secure, and how I learned to achieve this feeling was to disassociate myself from whatever situation I was in, stay silent and become invisible. My childhood logic told me that if I couldn't be heard, I couldn't be hurt, and I would be left alone. This same message was clearly coming from my inner child memories; I hadn't managed to reprogramme my thought process; and I knew it was time to do just that. The change was gradual. It didn't happen overnight; it took a lot of time, focus and reflection for me to recognise situations that triggered my behaviour. This meant I had to make myself visible, so I stopped shying away from conversations that from my own inadequacies overwhelmed me. I pushed myself to become visible, take centre stage and really start believing in myself, my skills, my abilities and my gift of communication. It was time to share the gift that I was given with those around me, and with the world.

Have you ever felt invisible? Do you allow yourself to hide who you really are, away from the world? Ask yourself why you do this, see if there is a pattern, and give yourself permission to retrace and track where that pattern started. You deserve to be visible; that is why you are here on this earth. It's time to change your previous behaviours and start setting your new intention. You are important, you are enough, so refuse to be invisible any longer. It's time to let people see who you really are.

Essential oils and meditation helped me to change my thought process and accept being visible in all situations, and they can assist you too. Purchase a 10ml rollerball bottle, fill it halfway with fractionated coconut oil, then add 25 drops of frankincense, 25 drops of lavender, 25 drops of bergamot and 5 drops of ginger. Apply this blend all over the front of your neck, across the top of your collar bone and in a straight line down the back of your neck. This blend of oils helped me let go of self-judgement and insecurities, all of which were keeping me in a space that I should have left a long time ago. I'm a firm believer that nothing happens before its time; if you feel this is your time then you are right. Start making the necessary changes one step at a time, and notice the subtle positive differences that you will start to experience, and that the people around you will recognise in you too.

Reinventing Your Wheel

Have you ever wondered how certain celebrities continually reinvent themselves? I remember that I used to assume it was only celebrities that could achieve this. They had a team of people that would create their new image and deliver the fully polished celebrity into the public eye. When I thought deeply about this and reflected on my own life's journey, I recognised that I had reinvented myself many times. Trade union workplace leader at age 17, fashion co-ordinator, senior manager, mother, business owner, natural health consultant, holistic coach and public speaker. As women, we are often seen through a narrow lens, as a mother, a wife, a caregiver, a career woman. In reality, we are many of these descriptors all at the same time. I've been blessed to have met so many women who seek me out for holistic coaching sessions. They may have gone through a divorce, a breakup of a long-term relationship, or redundancy, and consequently feel that they have lost their identity. We discuss the process of loss, change, and what it means to be single again.

Think about it this way: you have been given an incredible gift of redefining yourself. What do you identify with? Are you a dreamer or an independence seeker? Life can take you wherever you want to go, but you must start believing in yourself again. Nobody can change your past; your past belongs to you, and it shouldn't stop you from building and celebrating your future. In fact, reinventing yourself and learning to plan for the things you now have the freedom to do is incredibly powerful. You will always define your own terms when you reinvent yourself, and that's what it's all about. I'm not saying it's an easy process; it's all part of learning and accepting change and your new path.

This is a great essential oil recipe that may help you to redefine your own capabilities: In a 5ml rollerball bottle half full of fractionate coconut oil, blend together 25 drops of basil, 25 drops of wild orange, 15 drops of lemon, 15 drops of lime and 5 drops of peppermint. Once blended, roll onto the reflex points behind your ears, back of your neck, on your wrists or under the soles of your feet. This should help you feel more energetic, less lethargic, assist you with increased vitality, and reduce those feelings of fatigue. It's a beautiful citrus blend which you can also use as a natural perfume. It's all part of your reinvention process, and you will smell divine.

You can reinvent yourself as many times as you wish. There is no age limit, and it is not just for celebrities. Sometimes I hear my clients say, It's too late for me; I've missed my opportunity. This couldn't be further from the truth; it's never too late for change. If you want change, create it, and own it, just like you owned who you were previously. This time know that you have chosen who you are becoming and just enjoy the ride. Read on and you will find more helpful tips that you can incorporate into your daily life.

The Authentic You

What does the word authentic mean? The Oxford Dictionary definition it as follows: Of undisputed origin and not a copy; genuine. My interpretation of being authentic means embracing your true self, internally and externally. It is when your actions and words are congruent with your beliefs and values. It is being yourself, not an imitation of who you think you should be, or have been told you should be. There is no "should" in authentic. However, being authentic is not always an easy process. I remember being afraid of my own authenticity, and that was a result of my own insecurities. I told myself that I would not be accepted for who I truly was by others, and for many years found it easier to be who I thought other people wanted me to be, so I ignored my intuitive voice. I told myself that this suited me perfectly, when in reality I knew that I felt like a fraud, and I was only deceiving myself through not listening to my true calling.

I felt that I was no longer sure about who I was, and I knew that being an imposter to myself was extremely unfulfilling. When your spirituality continues to develop, and you truly start to understand who you are holistically, it becomes almost impossible to be unauthentic. Living unauthentically is both draining and tiring. I was always second-guessing what people thought about me, an unhelpful habit that I had formed over the years that was helping to keep me in a place of uncertainty.

The way I live my life today reflects my authenticity. I am who I am unapologetically; and those people that do not want to accept me for who I am are no longer in my life. It feels so much more empowering and purposeful. When I'm on stage sharing my story with hundreds of people, talking about my own vulnerabilities, flaws and imperfections, there is no better feeling as I know that the energy being shared in the room is pure, heartfelt and sincere.

Ask yourself this question: Am I living as my authentic self? If you are not, ask yourself why not. People are commonly drawn to others that exude authenticity. It takes time to stop seeking another person's approval, and that is different for each of us. When you reach that stage of your life, you will recognise for yourself that this is the only level of your identity that is real. The true, genuine substance of who you are is your authentic self. That is who you are at your absolute core. It is the part of you not designed or defined by your job, function or family role. It encompasses all your skills, talents, knowledge, gifts and ever-expanding wisdom.

Chapter 11

Transforming Your Joy Into
Your Newly Found Passion

Finding Your Joy

Reading through my book, I trust that you have learnt the basic steps of how to manifest what you want in your life. You may be wondering what I mean by finding your joy. I've already shared that it took time to find mine. For me it's very much about sharing the natural health message, embracing nature with every opportunity that I have. The feeling of satisfaction I get in return is remarkable. Inhaling, ingesting, diffusing or wearing pure therapeutic grade essential oils always puts a smile on my face, as does sharing them with other people. I have observed this reaction thousands of times; it's the smile on their faces, when they inhale these incredible essential oils, that really makes my heart jump for joy.

Happiness and joy are found within you. Start creating your own joyful story; rewrite your own book of pleasure. You can do this any time you please. The key is to take action, and experience small but meaningful changes. It may help if you journal your thoughts. What is it that makes you feel satisfied and fulfilled? What changes can you make now, to start moving toward those feelings? Has anybody ever said to you, if you find something that you love, and that you would do for free, consider developing your natural love into a business idea? I appreciate that this may not be immediately achievable for everyone, and you may need to tweak your idea. It's about what works best for you, and what keeps you energized and motivated, and ultimately feeling fulfilled with the path you have chosen.

You may be fully aware that you love working with people, and whatever it is that you do will need to involve supporting and helping others. Why not research and journal all the industries or roles that appeal to you in these areas? You may decide that you want to set up your own business helping other people. Acknowledge that any of these areas are possible for you; keep believing in yourself and moving towards your goal.

Most of all keep moving forward to become a better person, a better friend, a better parent in the world that surrounds you. It's very likely that you have achieved more than you give yourself credit for. After all, it's worth remembering that your life is not measured by the leaps and bounds you take, as much as by the little steps and decisions that you make every day without a second thought. Just by reading through this book, and absorbing new information and knowledge, you are already making progress, and making positive changes. Remember it's as much about the journey as it is about the end result; that's where the joy is discovered.

Sharing Your Gifts And Talents

Once I had a clear idea of what I wanted to do with the gifts that I had been blessed with, I knew I wanted to share the gift of emotional health and natural well-being with the world. But it didn't start that way. I initially wanted to share what I was learning about natural remedies only with my family and friends. On reflection, however, I realise I wasn't ready to take further action. I was dipping my toe in the water, which is also a good thing as I've already mentioned; it is about those small steps along the way. I believe, because of my interest and use of nature's medicine, my husband and I have been able to nourish ourselves holistically. The last time either of us visited the doctor with an illness or a condition was over 10 years ago; for our children around 6 years ago. I recognise that many people wish to seek help from their doctor for a range of ailments, and if you are under the doctor's consent then you must continue to do so. All I am doing is sharing this as part of my story, as it has been an integral part of revealing and sharing my contribution within my community.

The beautiful thing about imparting your gifts is that it comes naturally to you. It is not hard work, nor should it be It can be challenging to recognise the difference between work and doing what you love. Recently I was asked to speak at a women's empowerment seminar. this is an area that I love, as it's a great way to share the natural health message. Often, after I've finished my presentation, individuals will approach me and express how they felt motivated to improve their own health and change some of their less than helpful habits. This was due to what they heard me discuss whilst on the stage, and it's this that brings true joy and happiness to my heart.

I am thankful for being blessed with the gift of communication. At this particular event, it was early in the morning and a lady, who I shall call Jane, spoke to me and explained that she was suffering from fibromyalgia, chronic osteoporosis and sciatica. Jane was clearly in a lot of pain, so I gave her a blend of essential oils called Deep Blue Rub, which includes wintergreen, osmanthus, camphor, blue tansy, German chamomile and aloe vera leaf gel, all of which are highly anti-inflammatory. I asked Jane to use this topically on the area of inflammation. I had already ascertained that Jane had no form of skin sensitivity. By the end of the seminar, Jane approached me smiling, and informed me that her pain had reduced significantly. This was the first time she had been virtually pain free in the past two years and I was so pleased for her. As I observed her facial expressions, I knew that she would be able to experience a more enjoyable day. Jane was happier and, more importantly, was experiencing hope, and an opportunity to recognise that her health could improve over time.

Start sharing your gifts and talents. This was why they were given to you. It's about letting other people know that what you have to offer is precious and empowering. If you are unsure of what your gifts and talents are, and where you shine the brightest, don't be afraid to ask a good friend, or family member; someone who will be authentic, honest, supportive and positive whilst you're on your journey. Ask your friends to tell you what they see as your natural gifts and talents; this will probably reaffirm what you are already thinking. The world is waiting for you to share and shine.

Allowing Gratitude To Flourish

What does gratitude mean to you? Gratitude is a way of showing how thankful you are, for all that you have in your life. Even in challenging times, it's about counting your blessings and noticing the simple pleasures in life. It means learning to live your life with your eyes wide open, and not just focused on the day ahead and racing into that thought process. Gratitude informs you about how to shift your focus from what your life lacks to the abundance that is already present. There is abundance all around, but you may choose not to recognise it. But if you choose to acknowledge it, you will see that it has always been there; that it has always existed. Being thankful makes people happier and more resilient. It may strengthen relationships, and it helps to improve health and reduce stress. I wish to share another time in my life that I connected to my soul dots.

Back in 2012, I was at the gym participating in my weekly 6 am gruelling circuit training class. I recall jumping up with both feet and landing on two stacked stepper blocks, fully in my concentration zone. Without warning, I felt an excruciating pain penetrate through my ankle and my leg.

I was unable to walk, so I took a taxi to the hospital and I was informed that I had ripped my Achilles tendon. I had no option but to take time away from my job. This was the first time that I truly allowed myself to reflect on what I deemed as my failures and my achievements. This was life-changing for me. I started thinking deeply about how I showed gratitude, for what I already had, for where I had already been, for all the opportunities that had shown up in my life. Every day from that point, I started making more effort to recognise who and what was around me, and to be grateful for all the daily pleasures in my life. Although I was immobile for four months, I believe that my accident was a significant turning point in my life; it was another moment when I listened to my intuition. It forced me to stop and reflect on my life, and gave me the time and ability to imagine and create my positive new life plan.

Many people create a gratitude journal. It does not have to be a long and laborious process; it is a simple technique. This exercise consists of writing down, every day, a list of three things for which you feel grateful. You can do this first thing in the morning or before you go to bed at night. Work out which is the best time of day for you, as you want it to be consistent. Another idea for you to express gratitude is to write a gratitude letter to someone in your life who has been a positive influence, but whom you have not had the opportunity to thank appropriately.

As with anything new to your regime, to get started you will have to find what feels and works best for you. Once you become more familiar with completing your gratitude journal, you may notice that you concentrate far more on the good experiences, rather than the negative encounters that you may have held onto previously. This in turn may result in less stress and a more satisfying life.

The Path Of Alignment

We are all individuals, and it may take each of us a different time factor to fully understand why we are here, and what we are here to accomplish. Your time here is precious. All I request from you is that you listen and learn from the life lessons that you will experience. You may understand that, when you don't listen, generally you may encounter a more challenging lesson; eventually you may choose to listen and act accordingly.

People often talk about self-reflection; what does that mean to you? Until you truly meet and connect with yourself at a soul level, you may lack the ability to love yourself fully, and hence fully align yourself with your chosen path. Being spiritually aligned means discovering the essence of your being, who you really are, and the deepest values by which you live. You are ready to connect to a higher source of intelligence or power, identifying with something greater than the material world as you know it.

I acknowledge that I am still on my journey, and I'm not expecting it to end anytime soon. Every day for me is a new opportunity. Every day I embrace a few simple words: live, love, forgive, experience, and learn. These words are embedded as part of my life cycle. I believe that my life is a constant flow of experiences and memories, and I yearn to be the best that I can be. This is not to say that I don't have days where I'm feeling less energetic, and sometimes frustrated; however, these states of mind pass by quickly. I am able to reset my mind to ensure that I don't stay in that stuck, uncertain place any longer than necessary. Through meditation, I work on my thought process every day. When I wake up in the morning, I verbally express my gratitude for the day ahead; and before I go to sleep at night, I verbally give thanks for the day that I've experienced. I truly believe that, once you've set your intention and started to live your life on purpose, you will continue to follow through and find your true calling.

Your friends and family want the best for you; however, they can only see your world through their own eyes, and they will not have the same vision that you do. I want to highlight this, as I believe it is important to know that the people around you care about you deeply, but they are not you. Remember this, when you are in the throes of a heartfelt conversation with those who love you. Do not feel obliged to compromise your values or your dreams; they are yours for a reason.

You cannot change the world for the better until you decide to become the best version of yourself. This may take time, energy and a certain degree of hard work, depending on where you are on your journey right now. When you are intent on becoming your best self, naturally you will begin to evolve into a life filled with passion and purpose, which can only be achieved by living in the present moment.

Create Financial Health From Your Newly Found Passion

If you truly love what you do, investigate how you can create an income from your passion. When I retrained as a natural health and lifestyle coach and a clinical hypnotherapist, the training was the easy part. Once you leave your training colleagues and you're out there on your own for the first few months, it can feel very lonely. Whilst I was still in contact with my group, initially I was on my own. But I also felt a great sense of freedom, a great sense that I wanted to support and help other people. I had the skills and qualifications to do so, and that's exactly what I did. Shortly afterwards, I was introduced to these powerful essential oils and I experienced the butterfly feeling in my stomach. I recognised that intense intuitive feeling; these oils were much richer in quality than just aromatic smells; this was powerful plant medicine. I felt, deep down in my soul, that I wanted to educate people about plant medicine. I wasn't quite sure how at that time, but I felt very strongly about it. I know this may not happen for everybody; it's about following through and trusting your soul-felt intuition. I had spent a lot of money retraining. I followed my heart and my intuition, which had never let me down before. Currently I travel all over Europe, sharing the benefits of natural health. I consult with people all over the world who want to improve their quality of life. I shine a light with individuals and families that may have suffered with a variety of illnesses over a period of time.

This was not all smooth sailing; it's important to learn about the basics of running a business, and it's imperative if your passion is going to be successful and profitable. Be prepared to work at this. Success is not built overnight. There are low-cost and free business courses that you can research and then join. Generally, the course is for two to three days; this also gives you the opportunity to meet with other new up-and-coming business owners, so that you form part of a network, and in that way, you can support each other whilst embarking on these new challenges. Consider at times it may feel lonely, but in my experience, the joyful, heartfelt moments absolutely outweigh those times, and that's why it's important that you love your business. Otherwise during the challenging times, there is a danger that you may lose interest. Over time you will recognise that you have more flexibility, money, possibly a whole new group of friends, and a brand new network that you can tap into and share skills and new experiences. This may be an area that you need support with. You may require a coach to help you through this process; someone outside of your family or friends network to discuss sound business ideas with. Whatever it takes, start today, even if it's just writing down the ideas that have been ruminating in your mind; writing them down on paper is a great start.

Decide how big or small your creation will be. The safest way for you may be to work whatever your new idea is alongside your current job or business, in order that you understand the implications of what it takes to run a business. This is an effective way to set out; however, it's not for everybody. Some of my coaching clients are 100% committed from the offset. It very much depends on your thought process, how risk-averse you are, and your BELIEF mindset. You know you can do this. In fact, my intent is that this book has inspired you to start something new, no matter how small it may be.

Stand In Your Own Magnificence

As my journey continues, I recognise that I have built a strong foundation, and an appetite for transformational change. Every day I incorporate essential oils for healing, gratitude for life and living, and pray for continuous improvement in our world of both beauty and disaster. I've come to realise that living my life in its truest sense does not mean that my own imperfections will not try to regenerate, and re-establish themselves in my thought process. It's similar to mowing the garden lawn, and as part of the natural maintenance, revisiting every day to check if any weeds have started to push their way through the neat green blades of grass. I do the same in my life. I know that life is fluid, it rarely stands still, and this may be similar for you. As your foundation grows from strength to strength you will find it becomes much easier. As the late Maya Angelou once said, "Nothing can dim the light that shines from within." I've learnt how to appreciate my own magnificence. I no longer shy away from it as I did in my past; I feel so much happier walking towards it. I give myself what I need, and I acknowledge that it is safe for me to continue growing. The more fulfilled I am, the more love I have to share with all the people that I will meet on my journey of life.

This is your time right here in the present, so allow yourself to embrace your own imperfections as they are unique to you. Refrain from viewing them as if they are not worthy of your own recognition; instead, work with them and fully integrate them with who you really are.

When you embrace nature and live in the present, you will start to notice more frequently that your thoughts of joy and happiness and being grateful for what you have received will help to elevate your life.

To help you stand continuously in your own magnificence, you may wish to practice one or more of these daily affirmations:

- I live in the present and I am confident of the future.
- I am self-reliant, persistent, and creative in whatever I do.
- My personality shines with confidence; I am bold and outgoing.
- I always see the good in others; I attract only positive people.

If you would like to add another layer to your continued magnificence, include your therapeutic grade essential oils. Blend two drops of grapefruit, two drops of bergamot, and one drop of peppermint into your diffuser, or into the palm of your hands. Cup your hands together and inhale. Remember that citrus oils are both uplifting and motivating for your mood, and peppermint is effective for clearing your airways and supporting with focus and concentration.

Do not put off until tomorrow what you can initiate today; remember to enjoy your unique journey. Keep shining your light on your life, and all those people that you will meet along the way. When you look back at where you started, only then will you recognise how far you have come.

About The Author

Abi Osho is an award-winning author, international natural health & wellbeing coach, motivational speaker and leadership mentor. Abi has been using natural medicine for over 25 years, and is a true advocate of holistic health. Abi came from humble beginnings, and as a child was raised in foster care in East Sussex. She moved to London 30 years ago, and is married with 2 children.

Abi was a senior manager for over 20 years, and helped hundreds of young people and adults gain qualifications and secure employment. After going on her own journey of emotional healing, she decided that her true passion and purpose was to help people to heal emotionally, so she left a very promising career, followed her intuitive passion and retrained as a certified lifestyle coach, qualified clinical hypnotherapist, essential oil consultant and a certified NLP practitioner.

You will find Abi speaking regularly at seminars, workshops and radio shows about the power of natural plant-based medicines, living abundantly, and emotional health, as well as teaching her own classes and workshops across Europe.

In her book you will read many practical tips and helpful suggestions on how to improve your emotional health and physical wellbeing the natural way. She talks about exploring your natural surroundings, helpful nutrition tips, essential oils that support a range of conditions, her own painful experience of suffering from Carpal Tunnel Syndrome for 13 years, and how she overcame it naturally. She travels all over the world giving motivational talks.

Abi shares the highs and lows of her own journey to self-acceptance. You will find guidance on how to be courageous enough to listen to your inner voice and follow your own path whilst going through your transformational change, and knowing that the path of abundance is already yours.

You can find Abi Osho Founder of Soul Medicine on Facebook @soulmedicinedoterra, Instagram abi_soulmedicine, Youtube and LinkedIn. To find out how to purchase these incredible dōTERRA essential oils visit her doTERRA website below.

Abi is available to deliver motivational talks, presentations, keynote speeches, TV and radio appearances to the appropriate audiences in the UK, Europe and worldwide. For rates and availability, please find contact details below:

Email: abi@soul-medicine.co.uk
Website:www.soul-medicine.co.uk
www.mydoterra.com/soulmedicine

To order more books individually or in bulk please visit www.amazon.co.uk

Finally, if you have been inspired by this book, then share the gift that you have received and buy a copy for someone in your life who will also benefit as you did. Pass your positive energy forward.

STAY IN TOUCH WITH ABI OSHO
– RECEIVE YOUR FREE BONUS GIFT

Once you have purchased my book via my website or on Amazon, you will receive a FREE e-book about how to use dōTERRA essential oils. I would love to stay connected with you. I have coached hundreds of clients over the past 15 years, around the world. If you would like to find out how I can support you during your time of transition, please contact me. You will receive a FREE 20 minute skype call and 10% discount on my Experience, Embrace or Live, Soul Medicine coaching packages. Invite me to give a lunchtime guided relaxation class at your workplace or to speak at your annual event. To find out how you can purchase these incredible essential oils visit my dōTERRA website below:

Email: abi@soul-medicine.co.uk
Website: www.soul-medicine.co.uk
Website:www.mydoterra.com/soulmedicine

You can find Abi Osho on Facebook @soulmedicinedoterra, Instagram abi_soulmedicine, Youtube and LinkedIn
Soul Medicine: Love, Learn, Forgive, Experience, Live
Holistic Healing, every day the natural way

Stay connected with Abi go to
www.soul-medicine.co.uk
www.mydoterra.com/soulmedicine
Soul Medicine: Love, Learn, Forgive, Experience, Live
Holistic Health, everyday the natural way
#naturesmedicine#soulmedicine#melaninrising#selflove

32163933R00089

Printed in Poland
by Amazon Fulfillment
Poland Sp. z o.o., Wrocław